Orléans 1429

France turns the tide

OSPREY
PUBLISHING

Orléans 1429

France turns the tide

David Nicolle • Illustrated by Graham Turner

Series editor Lee Johnson • Consultant editor David G Chandler

First published in Great Britain in 2001 by Osprey Publishing, Elms Court, Chapel Way, Botley, Oxford OX2 9LP, United Kingdom. Email: info@ospreypublishing.com

ISBN 1 84176 232 6

Editor: Lee Johnson
Design: The Black Spot
Index by Alison Worthington
Maps by The Map Studio
3D bird's eye views by The Black Spot
Battlescene artwork by Graham Turner
Originated by Grasmere Digital Imaging, Leeds, UK
Printed in China through World Print Ltd.

01 02 03 04 05   10 9 8 7 6 5 4 3 2 1

For a catalogue of all books published by Osprey Military and Aviation please contact:

The Marketing Manager, Osprey Direct UK, PO Box 140, Wellingborough, Northants, NN8 4ZA, United Kingdom. Email: info@ospreydirect.co.uk

The Marketing Manager, Osprey Direct USA, c/o Motorbooks International, PO Box 1, Osceola, WI 54020-0001, USA. Email: info@ospreydirectusa.com

www.ospreypublishing.com

Author's Dedication

In memory of Air Vice Marshal Moustafa Shalabi el-Hinnawy, a genial warrior who helped turn the tide for Egypt.

Artist's note

Readers may care to note that the original paintings from which the colour plates in this book were prepared are available for private sale. All reproduction copyright whatsoever is retained by the Publishers. All enquiries should be addressed to:

Graham Turner
'Five Acres'
Buslins Lane,
Chartridge, Chesham,
Bucks,
HP5 2SN
United Kingdom

The Publishers regret that they can enter into no correspondence upon this matter.

KEY TO MILITARY SYMBOLS

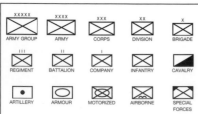

CONTENTS

FRANCE AND ENGLAND, 1429

Bristol
London
ENGLAND
Southampton
Dover
Calais
Ghent
Antwerp
FLANDERS
Brussels
BRABANT
English Channel
ARTOIS
Lille
Namur
HAINAUT
Cherbourg
Amiens
LUXEMBURG
PICARDY
RETHEL
Bayeux
Rouen
Caen
Reims
THE
EMPIRE
NORMANDY
Seine
CHAMPAGNE
Paris
Vaucouleurs
Verneuil
Domrémy
1424
BRITTANY
Chartres
Châteaudun
Seine
Rennes
MAINE
Orléans
Marne
Angers
Jargeau
Besançon
Baugé
Blois
Gien
Loire
1421
Tours
Beaugency
Cravant
Dijon
ANJOU
C. OF
1423
Chinon
TOURAINE
Bourges
NEVERS
BURGUNDY
Poitiers
Nevers
(DUCHY)
(COUNTY)
BERRY
POITOU
BOURBON
Bay
of
Loire
Saône
Biscay
LIMOUSIN
Auvergne
SAVOY
Lyons
Grenoble
Bordeaux
Dordogne
Cévennes
DAUPHINE
Lot
Rhône
Garonne
Avignon
ARMAGNAC
PROVENCE
Toulouse
NAVARRE
Pyrenees
ARAGON
Mediterranean
Sea

Rhine
Meuse
Moselle
Rhône

Territory recognising King Henry VI (of England)
as king of France.

Territory recognising the Dauphin (subsequently King)
Charles VII as uncrowned king of France.

Not recognising the 'English' or the Burgundians
but not necessarily recognising the Dauphin either.

Burgundian land outside the Kingdom of France
(inside the Empire).

Burgundian land inside France and recognising
King Henry VI as king of France.

Taken by the English under the Earl of Salisbury
in 1428.

N

0   100 miles

0   100 km

ORIGINS OF THE CAMPAIGN

In 1415 King Henry V of England invaded France, taking advantage of the insanity of the French king Charles VI and a civil war between two competing factions within France – the Armagnacs and the Burgundians. The astonishing success of the invasion also strengthened Henry V's own position in England since he was regarded by many as the son of a usurper. Henry V's invasion was, of course, part of the ongoing Hundred Years War in which English kings fought to establish their claim to be legitimate kings of France as well. Before 1415 the English had, however, effectively lost the war but after their overwhelming victory at Agincourt – a victory which virtually wiped out the Armagnac leadership – the English went on to conquer a large part of northern France.

Meanwhile Charles, the Valois Dauphin or heir apparent who would eventually lead a French revival, was an inexperienced youth. Uncertain of his abilities and even of the legitimacy of his own cause, he retreated south to the little town of Bourges. His political and military career really started when he became Lieutenant Governor of those parts of France that escaped English invasion and had not been taken over by the Burgundians. For their part the rulers of Burgundy were in a strange position, holding huge swathes of territory in eastern France, where they acknowledged the French Crown, and also in the neighbouring German

Orléans with its Cathedral and the 18th-century Pont George V, which replaced the medieval bridge 100 metres (328ft) upriver. (author's photograph)

Wall painting of 'The Martyrdom of St. Thomas of Canterbury' at the head of King Henry IV's tomb in Canterbury Cathedral, as reconstructed by Prof. E.W. Tristram. It illustrates the sort of armour that the English would have worn during the siege of Orléans.

Empire, where they acknowledged the supremacy of the Emperor.

It was a complex situation in which the widely despised young Dauphin Charles tried to resist English conquest and also allowed his Armagnac supporters to assassinate Duke John of Burgundy – an action which encouraged the Burgundians into an alliance with the English. Then in 1420 King Charles VI of France agreed to the Treaty of Troyes in an effort to end the war. Henry V was to marry Charles VI's daughter and their child would be heir to the thrones of both France and England. The unfortunate Dauphin Charles in Bourges was disinherited. When England and Burgundy signed a formal alliance the story seemed to be at an end.

In 1421, however, the Dauphin's troops won a notable victory at Baugé, though this was not followed up. Next year Henry V of England and Charles VI of France both died. According to the Treaty of Troyes the infant King Henry VI of England now became King of France, but the Treaty of Troyes had not been recognised outside those areas controlled by the English and Burgundians. As a result the country was divided into two; so-called 'Lancastrian France', which recognised Henry VI and was actually ruled by Henry VI's Regent, the Duke of Bedford, based in Paris assisted by his Burgundian allies, and 'Valois France', which recognised the Dauphin, who now claimed to be King Charles VII. Bedford sincerely wanted the French people to accept Henry VI as their king and there were, in fact, many in northern and eastern France who did so. They, like the English and Burgundians, claimed that Charles was a rebel who had been disinherited by his own father. Charles VII's position was further weakened because he could not have a proper coronation in the traditional cathedral at Reims, which lay within Anglo-Burgundian territory.

Though there was fighting during these confused years, the struggle was primarily diplomatic. Brittany, for example, sometimes joined the English and the Burgundians in a triple alliance while at other times its dukes supported Charles VII in southern France. Charles VII and his advisors also worked to undermine the Anglo-Burgundian axis. On the other hand the English and Burgundians won notable victories and stabilised a frontier between Anglo-Burgundian and 'Valois' France roughly along the River Loire. Bedford usually had about 15,000 troops scattered in garrisons and sieges. Nevertheless, pro-Valois enclaves survived as far away as the frontier with the German Empire and even the English hold on Paris sometimes looked vulnerable. On the other hand both the attempts by Charles's army to

A mid-15th-century illustration of the assassination of Duke John the Fearless of Burgundy by the Dauphin Charles's Armagnac supporters. This murder drove the Burgundians into an alliance with the English. (*Chronicle of Enguerrand de Monstrelet*, Bib. Arsenal, Ms. 5084, f.1, Paris)

open the road to Reims were defeated, first at Cravant in 1423 and the latter at Verneuil 1424.

Charles VII was certainly not the feeble character portrayed in English popular literature. True he was unmilitary, far from warlike and lacked self-confidence. Yet Charles VII ended up as one of the most effective French rulers in the later medieval period. He was quiet, solitary, hard working, sober and, as a youth, was described as morose, but he had a keen sense of humour and liked the ladies as well as playing chess and hunting with the crossbow. Unfortunately he was also perpetually short of money to pay his troops.

Deprived of his closest relatives by death or captivity, Charles was surrounded by competing advisors. Many were unscrupulous schemers but they were often competent and strong minded. Arthur de Richmont the Constable, for example, was an excellent soldier but, dismissed in disgrace at the end of 1427, had fled to Brittany. Charles VII's marriage to Mary of Anjou also provided him with a formidable mother-in-law. She was Yolande of Aragon, a woman whose role in the struggle against the English invaders was almost as important as that of Jeanne d'Arc – though very different. Charles and his advisors may not have appeared heroic, while his military commanders were often little better than bandits, but between them they kept the Valois cause alive and stopped the English from taking over the whole country. When Jeanne d'Arc burst upon the scene in 1429 she found soldiers and a king ready to be inspired by her remarkable vision of liberation.

CHRONOLOGY

1428

July, English army under the Earl of Salisbury sails from Southampton to Harfleur then marches to Paris.

August, English army under Salisbury marches from Paris to Chartres.

8 September, English under Salisbury capture Meung.

26 September, English under Salisbury capture Beaugency.

5 October, English under Salisbury capture Jargeau.

6 October, English under Salisbury capture Châteauneuf.

12 October, English begin siege of Orléans.

24 October, Salisbury killed in Les Tourelles by cannon fire.

24 October–15 April 1429, English construct siege positions (*bastilles* & *boulevards*) around Orléans.

8 November, French defenders of Orléans destroy 13 churches outside the walls of the city.

29 December, French defenders of Orléans destroy the remaining six churches outside the walls.

30 December, Dunois leads unsuccessful sortie against the English outside Orléans.

1429

15 January, Dunois leads unsuccessful sortie against the English outside Orléans.

February, Large English supply column under Sir John Fastolf leaves Paris to support the besiegers outside Orléans.

11 February, French force under Clermont and La Hire link up in an attempt to intercept the English supply column.

12 February, English defeat French at the Battle of the Herrings near Rouvray; Clermont retreats to Tours.

23 February–6 March, Jeanne d'Arc travels from Vaucouleurs to see Charles VII at Chinon.

March–April, Jeanne d'Arc sent to Poitiers for interrogation, then returned to Tours.

20 April, English build their final fortified siege position (Bastille de Saint-Jean-le-Blanc) south-east of Orléans.

21–24 April, Jeanne d'Arc goes from Tours to Blois, where Charles VII's army has assembled and is joined by Dunois and La Hire.

24–27 April, Jeanne d'Arc sends a letter to the English, warning them to abandon their siege.

26 April, Jeanne d'Arc and the French army leave Blois and march towards Orléans.

29 April, Large supply column with a covering force crosses the Loire.

30 April, La Hire leads Orléans militia in an unsuccessful attack on the English Boulevard of Saint-Pouair; Jeanne d'Arc goes to the end of the broken Loire bridge and urges Sir William Glasdale to abandon the siege.

1 May, Dunois goes to Blois to confer with Clermont and collect additional troops; Jeanne d'Arc and her companions ride around Orléans, encouraging the people.

2 May, Jeanne d'Arc and her companions ride outside Orléans to view the English siege-works.

3 May, Religious processions throughout Orléans.

4 May, Dunois returns with additional troops along with La Hire and other leaders; a French force probably remains on the southern side of the Loire to watch the English siege-works; French in Orléans attack, overrun and dismantle the English Boulevard de Saint-Loup.

5 May, Jeanne d'Arc sends another letter to the English in Les Tourelles; French advance against the English Boulevard de Saint-Jean-le-Blanc; the English evacuate before the French arrive.

6 May, French attack and overrun the English siege position at the Boulevard des Augustins, near the southern end of the Loire bridge.

7 May, French attack the English-held bridge fortress of Les Tourelles, which falls after a full day's fighting; Jeanne d'Arc is wounded; Sir William Glasdale is killed.

7–8 May, French repair the broken bridge with timber.

8 May, English troops abandon their remaining siege fortifications then draw up for battle; French troops come out of Orléans and draw up for battle; the English withdraw towards Meung and Jargeau; some French troops attack the English rearguard.

8 June, English reinforcements under Sir John Fastolf leave Paris.

10 June, Jeanne d'Arc and the French advance from Orléans towards Jargeau.

12 June, French retake Jargeau; English reinforcements under Sir John Fastolf establish camp on Les Plaines de la Beauce near Janville.

15 June, Jeanne d'Arc and the French retake the bridge at Meung then march towards Beaugency, where they are joined by Arthur de Richemont and his Breton troops.

16 June, English under Fastolf march from Janville towards Meung and Beaugency.

17 June, Stand-off as French besieging Beaugency face English under Fastolf two kilometres (1¼ miles) from Beaugency; English withdraw to Meung; English garrison in Beaugency surrenders (night of 17/18 June).

18 June, English garrison allowed to leave Beaugency, then marches towards Janville; the main English force in Meung tries to retake the Loire bridge but fails so abandons Meung and retreats towards Janville; Jeanne d'Arc and the French army pursue the English; French cavalry vanguard under La Hire and Xaintrailles defeats the English at the battle of Patay; Talbot captured, Fastolf escapes.

17 July, Charles VII is crowned at Reims.

8 September, Jeanne d'Arc leads an unsuccessful attack on English-held Paris.

1430

24 May, Jeanne d'Arc captured by the Burgundians at Compiègne and is sold to the English.

1431

30 May, Jeanne d'Arc burned at the stake in English-ruled Rouen.

OPPOSING COMMANDERS

FRENCH LEADERS

Jeanne d'Arc was the dominant personality during the relief of Orléans but as yet she was rarely in command of French forces. In fact the leadership of French armies changed quite often. For example Jean, Comte de Dunois, was normally in charge in Orléans and probably commanded most attempts to break the siege. The field army at Blois was actually under the Maréchal de Broussac while the army which retook the English-held Loire towns after the relief of Orléans was commanded by the Duc d'Alençon.

Nevertheless, **Jeanne d'Arc** came to be seen as the French army's 'inspiration' – almost like a living banner. Born on 6 January 1412, Jeanne was not the simple shepherdess of popular legend but was one of the five children of Jacques d'Arc and Isabelle Romée, prosperous labourers in the village of Domrémy, which lay in the generally pro-Valois *châtellenie* of Vaucouleurs in eastern France. According to the Chronicles of Enguerrand de Montstrelet, when Jeanne d'Arc met Charles VII in Chinon: *She was dressed like a man … This Jeanne, the Maid, had for some time been chambermaid at an inn. She was also thoroughly used to riding horses and taking them to water, and could do other feats which girls do not usually do.* The young Duc d'Alençon described the dark-haired girl as beautiful. Her companions-in-arms generally called her 'La Pucelle' or the Maiden, and although Jeanne d'Arc was undoubtedly very pious she liked dancing. Her own philosophy of military leadership was simple, and could be summarised in her own words: *I used to say to them* [the soldiers], *'Go boldly in amongst the English,'* and then I used to go boldly in myself.

Jeanne's military skills seem to have come naturally, and Thomas Basin, author of the contemporary *Histoire de Charles VII*, described her wearing full armour: *Certainly everyone was astonished that this task was taken on by a girl of so tender an age, apart from being a young woman. So, in the fashion of a robust man experienced in the use of arms, she marched with the whole army, with her own personal banner ahead of her, on which was displayed the image of the glorious Virgin, Mother of God, and several other saints.* Alençon was also impressed by Jeanne's military abilities; *… in matter of war she was very expert, in the management of the lance as in the drawing up of an army in battle order and in preparing the artillery.* Furthermore: *… she acted so wisely and clearly in waging war, as if she was a captain who had the experience of twenty or thirty years, and especially in the setting up of artillery, for in that she held herself magnificently.*

In later years the concept of a female warrior came to be seen as exotic, but medieval attitudes were often closer to modern feminist ideas. Women of the French aristocracy were expected to take on some military responsibilities in their husband's absence. The French

The coat-of-arms conferred on Jeanne d'Arc by King Charles VII on 25 December 1429 following the successful campaign to relieve Orléans. (Ms. Fr. 5524, f.142, Bibliothèque Nationale, Paris)

The famous carved demons on the Cathedral of Notre Dame in Paris have looked down on various invaders for 700 years. In the early 15th century it was the English. Two years after this photograph was taken in 1938 it would be the Germans. (Patrick Nicolle photograph)

proto-feminist Christine de Pizan, who was still writing during Jeanne's lifetime, described how a woman should behave if she found herself in charge of a castle: *We have also said that she should have a man's heart, which means that she should know the laws of warfare and all things pertaining to them so that she will be prepared to command her men if there is need of it. She should try out her defenders and ascertain the quality of their courage and determination before putting too much trust in them … She must give special attention to what resources she would have until her husband could return …* The main difference was that Jeanne d'Arc came from a peasant background, not from the aristocratic warrior elite.

The other French leaders have been overshadowed by Jeanne and they, of course, never became Saints. **Jean II Duc d'Alençon**, for example, was aged 25 in 1429 and had just returned after five years in English captivity. His great-grandfather had been killed at Crécy, his father at Agincourt. On campaign Jean d'Alençon lived in very close proximity to Jeanne d'Arc, as he recalled during her rehabilitation trial several years after Jeanne was burned at the stake in Rouen: *Sometimes in the army I lay down to sleep with Jeanne and the other soldiers, all in the straw together, and sometimes I saw Jeanne prepare for the night and sometimes I looked at her breasts which were beautiful and yet I never had carnal desire for her …* In later years the Duc d'Alençon turned against Charles VII and was arrested for supposedly plotting with the English as well as indulging in black magic. Certainly this strange man was very superstitious, became a patron of astrologers and was one of those senior French noblemen who resisted King Charles VII's attempts to impose a centralised monarchy on France. His sentence of death was commuted to life imprisonment and Jean d'Alençon was eventually released when Charles VII's son Louis became king.

Another Jean, the **Comte de Dunois**, was generally known as The Bastard of Orléans. This brave, dedicated and skilful commander was the illegitimate son of Duc Louis d'Orléans. Born in 1403, he was recognised by his father and was thus accepted as a member of the French nobility. Indeed Jean de Dunois effectively became head of the Orléans dynasty after his legitimate half-brothers were captured at the battle of Agincourt. His military career began in 1417 when he was only 15 years old. Captured by the Burgundians himself, Jean the Bastard of Orléans spent two years in prison. In 1423 Charles VII made him Lieutenant General of the Kingdom and in this role he defeated the English at Montargis in 1427. As Charles's most successful commander, he was placed in charge of those few French troops equipped to maintain long campaigns. Most of Dunois's battles were victories, which was rare for French commanders at that time, but he was also very realistic and recognised the limitations of the forces under his command. He played a major role in French military reforms and commanded major elements of those armies which reconquered Normandy and Guyenne at the end of the Hundred Years War.

Some other French commanders and professional 'captains' came from humbler backgrounds. For example La Hire and Poton de Xaintrailles were described by Olivier de la Marche in his *Mémoires* as being masters of pillage and *escorchérie* or the ravaging of enemy and sometimes friendly lands, while at the same time being two of the most renowned of French commanders.

Born around 1390, Étienne de Vignolles came, like so many famous French soldiers, from Gascony. Nicknamed **La Hire** or 'The Hedgehog' because of his prickly temper, he was first recorded in a command role around 1420. Thereafter he took part in defeats and victories. In fact La Hire's greatest success was in maintaining an army in the field despite disasters – and often despite the cost to those he served. La Hire's bandit-like behaviour was, however, overshadowed by his service alongside Jeanne d'Arc, who made a hero of this rough and ruthless fighting man. He swore a lot and prayed a lot, though his prayers sometimes sounded like swearing. On at least one occasion he was reported as praying: *Lord God, I pray you to do for La Hire what La Hire would do for you if God was a captain and La Hire was God.* La Hire's oaths were proverbial and when Jeanne banned swearing in the French army she allowed a small concession to La Hire, permitting him to swear 'In the Name of God!' by 'By my staff!' Eventually he became the *bailli* of Vermandois and died in the presence of his king after a remarkably long and colourful military career.

Poton de Xaintrailles was another Gascon of obscure family background. Like La Hire, Poton de Xaintrailles and his less well-known brother were professional soldiers whose sometimes brutal careers have been glamorised by their association with Jeanne d'Arc. He was also a keen and successful participant in the jousting tournaments which become a noble sport in late medieval France. One of the earliest references to Poton de Xaintrailles was in 1421 when he fought for the Dauphin against the Burgundians and captured the castle of Le Crotoy. At that time he was described merely as a valiant squire. When the

Many professional soldiers in the army of Charles VII had humble origins and, in effect, rose from the ranks. They were often illiterate and only learned to sign their names later in life. The difficulty this caused them is obvious in the signatures of Poton de Xaintrailles, made in 1460 when he was a Marshal of France (1) and Étienne de Vignolles, called La Hire (2). (P.O. 2356, dossier Saintrailles no. 39, Bibliothèque Nationale, Paris, and Collège Française de Beaucorps, Paris)

Dauphin's army was defeated by the Burgundians at Mons-en-Vimeu, Poton was captured and imprisoned, but was soon released and was campaigning in the same area a few years later.

Poton de Xaintrailles had no illusions about being a courtier. In fact he took pride in being a mere soldier, saying of himself and those like him: *We are not of the court and the council. We are of the field of battle.* Xaintrailles first met Jeanne d'Arc when King Charles sent her to the army at Blois. He then remained her faithful companion-in-arms, being captured with Jeanne outside Compiègne in 1431. Since Poton was captured by the Earl of Warwick, and it had been one of Xaintrailles's retinue who had captured Warwick's son-in-law Talbot at the battle of Patay two years earlier, an exchange was arranged. Over the following years Poton de Xaintrailles was made King Charles VII's Grand Écuyer before becoming a Marshal of France in 1454. The old soldier continued to serve Charles's son, Louis XI, and was still leading troops in 1461 when he was over 70 years of age.

The division between soldiers and diplomats was not clear cut and one of those who served in both capacities was **Raoul V de Gaucourt**. He was first mentioned in 1411 in the entourage of the Comte d'Armagnac. In 1415 he defended Harfleur against Henry V and spent ten years as a prisoner of the English. He then re-entered Charles VII's service and was credited with thwarting a supposed rebellion by Arthur de Richemont. Gaucourt subsequently combined the positions of Captain of Chinon and Master of the Royal Household. He was also governor of Orléans, responsible for strengthening its defences before the siege began, and remained its governor during the early part of the siege. Nevertheless, de Gaucourt was at Chinon when Jeanne d'Arc arrived and his wife, Jeanne de Naillac, niece of the famous Philibert de Naillac who became Master of the Order of the Hospitallers, was one of those ladies who checked Jeanne d'Arc's virginity. Though claiming to have been impressed by Jeanne d'Arc, Raoul de Gaucourt always seems to have been lukewarm towards her.

De Gaucourt was later a member of the delegation that negotiated a truce with the English, having by then decided that Jeanne d'Arc had outlived her usefulness. He was also one of the men chosen by Charles VII to start reorganising the French army in 1439. Raoul was still seigneur of Gaucourt in 1446, by which time this old and highly experienced leader had earned his reputation as one of the most remarkable men of the time.

ENGLISH LEADERS

English military historians have tended to forget English military leaders who lose. However, this has been less true of those unlucky men who found themselves facing French armies inspired by the presence of Jeanne d'Arc. The first English commander during the siege of Orléans was the Earl of Salisbury, but he was killed almost at the outset. The man who took over was **William de la Pole, Earl of Suffolk**. The De La Pole family had a humble background, being descended from a Hull merchant, and although they became wealthy and played a leading role in the affairs of 15th-century England, the older noble families rarely let the De La Poles forget their origins.

William, the 4th Earl and 1st Duke of Suffolk, spent many years as an English commander in France. But his military career was so dogged by bad luck that many believed the Fates were against him. Nevertheless, William de la Pole, Earl of Suffolk was a brave, sincere and tenacious commander though lacking in charisma and a poor judge of character. After his defeats at the hands of Jeanne d'Arc, Suffolk abandoned the battlefield in favour of politics. In 1430 he married Alice, the widow of his old comrade-in-arms Salisbury and together they founded a college of priests at Ewelme in Oxfordshire. As Steward of the Royal Household and then as Lord Great Chamberlain, Suffolk became indispensable to the young King Henry VI. He dominated home and foreign affairs in the 1440s but, as English fortunes went from bad to worse, Suffolk became extremely unpopular. He was eventually impeached and then murdered on his way into exile in 1450.

Sir John Fastolf was luckier. Born around 1378, and dying nine years after Suffolk, this English soldier enjoyed a distinguished if ultimately

Statue of St. Michael in typical French mid-15th-century armour. (*in situ* Church of St. Roman, Locronan, Brittany)

unsuccessful military career in France. One of the first references to John Fastolf was in November 1415 when he led a raid to within a few kilometres of Rouen. He later captured the Duc d'Alençon at the battle of Verneuil, was promoted to the rank of knight and received a substantial grant of French land. He then played a major role during a campaign into the Maine area of western France and became a member of the prestigious Order of the Garter in 1426.

Three years later, during the Orléans campaign, Sir John Fastolf was at the height of his fame. As a military commander he carefully assessed risks, acted accordingly, was often quite cautious and was aware of the varied quality of his troops. Nevertheless, Fastolf's name was greatly respected amongst his French opponents. His defeat at the battle of Patay and his apparent abandonment of Talbot, who was captured by the French, resulted in him being stripped of his Order of the Garter though this was returned a few years later. Unfairly accused of reducing the strength of English garrisons in Normandy, Fastolf was in reality one of those leaders who wanted to extract England honourably from an impossible situation. Brave and capable, but grasping and merciless in the administration of his large estates in England, Fastolf also contributed towards the building of philosophy schools in Cambridge University and endowed Magdalen College at Oxford University.

Born around 1380, **John Lord Talbot** was known during his lifetime as 'The English Achilles' and latterly became the Earl of Shrewsbury. Soon after the accession of Henry V he was made Lieutenant of Ireland with the title of Sir John Talbot Lord Furnival. In 1417 he was one of the leaders of the English army which captured the Norman city of Caen. Though loyal, with iron determination and great courage, he was not a very good general and seemed to lack foresight. He lost his two major battles, Patay where he was captured and Castillon where he was killed. Nor was Lord Talbot a good team-player, being obstinate and over-confident. Nevertheless he was an inspiring leader whose luck held while the English were winning. In fact his name became a rallying cry for the English: *The cry of Talbot, serving for a sword! The scourge of France! The Talbot so feared abroad that with his name the mothers stilled their babes!*

Sir Thomas Scales came from a prominent political family in England. In 1423 he was appointed Captain General of the Seine towns, charged with preventing Armagnac raiders crossing the river. The following year he took part in the great English victory at Verneuil and in 1425 he and Fastolf were sent to take control of Maine. Here Scales seems largely to have been remembered for the way he organised the distribution of prisoner ransoms following the capture of Le Mans. Like Talbot, Scales was a very decisive commander but never became so famous. Captured at Patay, he was later released and won a small but notable victory over his old opponent La Hire at Ry in Normandy in 1436. When the English civil Wars of the Roses broke out, Scales was a leading supporter of the Lancastrian cause. Captured yet again when the Tower of London fell in 1460, Sir John was granted his freedom but was murdered on his way to find sanctuary in Westminster.

The English officer who had the closest and best documented dealing with Jeanne d'Arc at the siege of Orléans was **Sir William Glasdale**. As Sir William Glansdale he even has a line and a half of dialogue in Shakespeare's play *King Henry VI, Part One*. Nothing seems to be known of his origins, though his name might indicate that his family came from the poor and rugged region of Glaisdale in the North York Moors. Sir William took part in the Cravant campaign of 1423. After this victory, Salisbury sent a column under the Earl of Suffolk as far as Mâcon, deep into the heart of Burgundy. There Suffolk detached a force under Captain Sir William Glasdale to penetrate even further south to capture the strong castle of La Roche. Another Glasdale named Sir Gilbert, perhaps a relative, was Salisbury's lieutenant in the Mâcon area in 1423 where he led a contingent of 62 men-at-arms and 149 archers.

William Glasdale seems to have been present at the victory of Verneuil, probably in Suffolk's retinue. He also seems to have taken part in Suffolk's capture of Jargeau in October 1428. Glasdale was certainly with the main English army which camped near the southern end of the Orléans bridge on 12 October 1428. Here a French poem, *Le Mistère d'Orléans*, written a short while later, has Glasdale bemoan the death of the Earl of Salisbury, describing Salisbury as: *He, who had made and sustained all our host through his valiance, and who knew full well how to conquer all of France*. When Suffolk took over command following the death of Salisbury he put Sir William Glasdale in charge of the vital fortress of Les Tourelles. There he would eventually be killed when Jeanne d'Arc's followers captured the place.

OPPOSING ARMIES

THE FRENCH ARMY

The French army had, not surprisingly, suffered a marked decline after its catastrophic defeat at the battle of Agincourt. During the last years of King Charles VI 'The Mad' and the early years of Charles VII the royal staff that supervised and regulated the contracting of troops fell into near anarchy. Meanwhile the financial crisis grew even worse. Many sources of royal revenue were seized by powerful princes and the royal currency was steadily devalued. As a result the few troops whom King Charles VII could call upon were not always paid and often had to live off the land. During the siege of Orléans the difficulty of paying troops became quite serious. For example the Sire de Coarze, Hémon Raguier, and his men often seem to have received only one-third of their proper allowance, which of course caused problems between the garrison and local merchants. On the other hand the troops did get grants of food and wine, perhaps instead of pay.

A series of defeats also wiped out many of Charles VII's allied Scottish troops and all that was available in 1428–29 were garrisons loyal to the Armagnac cause, urban militias, free companies loyal to their own leadership, and some foreign mercenaries. The result was a war of small forces in which the French had so far achieved little. Considering the relatively small number of troops engaged, the number of captains in Charles VII's service was large. Those mentioned in the anon-

The Lords (upper) and Commons (lower) in the English parliament of King Henry VI as shown in a 15th-century manuscript. (*Foundation Charter of King's College,* King's College Library, Ms. Mun. KC-18-N1, Cambridge)

The stern castle of Châteaudun survived as an almost isolated outpost of territory loyal to Charles VII throughout the Orléans campaign. It was garrisoned by Dunois's troops and the rectangular wing to the left of the tall tower is, in fact, credited to Jean, Comte de Dunois. (Château de Châteaudun photograph)

ymous *Journal du siège d'Orléans* at the very start of that siege included Raymon de Villar, the Sire de Guitry or Guillaume de Chaumont, the Sire de Courras, also known as Coarze de Béarn, Poton de Xaintrailles and his brother Mathias or Macias d'Archac, Pierre de la Chapelle and the governor of the city, Raoul de Gaucourt. Most of these names appeared again in a muster list of 30 September. La Hire and Bernard de Comminges were absent, though their troops were in Orléans. Charles VII, meanwhile, relied on a few captains who had proved themselves loyal, while many of the others were little better than bandit chiefs.

The units commanded by such men were again very small. This was apparent in treasury documents relating to their pay, for example on 30 October 1428: *To Monseigneur the Bastard of Orléans* [Dunois], *12 men-at-arms and 2 archers etc, one hundred and four livres tournois.* It is worth noting that such payments were often in reliable *livres tournois* rather than in the often devalued royal *livres.*

As the English approached the Loire, an effort was made to summon those holding fiefs on a feudal basis but this did not produce many troops. Other men may have been pressed into service. But the most effective troops were now professional volunteers, mostly French but including Scots and other foreigners. Many of these professionals were based near Charles VII's capital or were garrisoning frontier fortifications. Other mercenaries were newly recruited. For example in February 1429 the King gave 3,750 *livres tournois* to four captains so that they could recruit men-at-arms and crossbowmen to relieve Orléans.

Wall painting of the sons and daughters of the lord of St. Floret made between 1415 and 1425. This region of south-central France remained loyal to the Valois cause and its local knightly class may well have served in the armies of Charles VII. (*in situ* church, St. Floret; author's photograph)

'The Town Garden', in a 15th-century French manuscript of *Le Livre de Prouffiz Ruraulx* by Crescentius. Medieval gardens tended to be very formal, often with raised beds and very intensive methods of cultivation. Those walled gardens inside a city under siege would inevitably have converted to food production as soon as supplies ran short. (Brit Library, Ms. Add. 19720, f.165, London)

The system of indenture, as used on the English side, seems to have been abandoned in France. Instead Charles VII accepted the services of established war chiefs who already had troops available. Perhaps as a result, these war chiefs were often very difficult for Charles's government and senior commanders to control. This was, of course, one of the main reason why Charles VII embarked on a process of thorough military reform once his position was assured, but that was long after the end of the Orléans campaign.

The captains themselves were a mixed group. Most were French but of the 65 listed by Hémon Raguier in March and April 1429 none came from the upper aristocracy. Only 28 were knights and the rest were either squires or had no noble rank at all. In fact there seem to have been only 40 knights in the entire army, in stark contrast to the aristocratic French army defeated at Agincourt 14 years earlier. Some of the captains came from regions already lost to the English. There were also many Bretons, despite the official neutrality of their Duke, while others came from those regions of southern France under Charles VII's rule. The foreign captains included Lombards from Italy, Aragonese from Spain and some Scotsmen. In fact foreign soldiers may have formed a full quarter of Charles VII's army.

The types of troops were less varied than their origins. The most important were fully armoured men-at-arms who fought primarily as cavalry but were also fully prepared to fight on foot. It is interesting to note that although the 10 to 17 year-old pages who looked after these men-at-arms did not normally take part in battle, they organised themselves to challenge opposing English pages during the siege of Orléans. The resulting stone-throwing 'battles' were recorded in the *Journal* on 3 and 4 April 1429, causing one death and many injuries.

Most of the infantry on the French side were either professional crossbowmen or longbowmen, or urban militiamen. The bulk of the latter were armed with assorted staff weapons, though they also included crossbowmen and archers. The local defence of Orléans itself seems to have been reorganised in 1417 by the then governor, Robert de Monroe. The walls were divided into six sections, each under an officer called a *cinquantenier* who commanded five *dizainiers* and a total of 50 men. Next year the governor checked their military equipment but there seems no evidence that militia crossbowmen served as units in return for tax exemption, as was the case in northern France. French urban militias were largely drawn from poor artisans, many of whom were below the tax threshold. Theoretically they were unpaid, though in reality they often received money. Commanded by a town consul, town captain or a prominent citizen, they had their own trumpeter and perhaps a flag. Many towns also recruited some professional soldiers.

Artillery played a major role on both sides and by the 1420s cannon were reliable enough to change the character if not the outcome of sieges. There was also an increasing number of smaller guns called *culverins*, which were highly effective as anti-personnel weapons. French urban fortification steadily improved during the Hundred Years War. The importance of the *capitaines de villes* who were in military charge of such places similarly increased, along with the resources allocated to them. Within towns there was a remarkable lack of resistance to high tax demands to be spent on such things as fortifications. In fact, the

'The capture of King John of France by the English at the battle of Poitiers', as shown in an early 15th-century French manuscript. The military equipment is typical of the period when the painting was made. (*Chroniques de Froissart*, Mss. 864-865, Bib. Municipale, Besançon)

strengthening of walls, towers and gates reflected the prestige of a city while also demonstrating that it was a safe place in which to trade. In urban architectural terms, the Age of Cathedrals had apparently been followed by the Age of Fortification.

The fortifications of Orléans were amongst the strongest in Valois France and the city's guns were large. Some fired cannonballs weighing almost 90 kilos (200lb). During the siege one even tried to hit a boat linking English siege-works north and south of the Loire – a moving target about a kilometre ($2/3$mile) away. In 1418 the governor of Orléans inspected the defences and ordered the construction of *bouloarts* or *boulevards* in front of each gate. These were separate field fortifications made of stone, timber and fascines embanked with earth. Next year mobile wooden barriers were erected ahead of these *boulevards* to protect the suburbs. More permanent defences included at least one stone *barbican* between Porte Paris and Tour Jehan Thibaut. In the *fosse* in front of all or most of the gates was a *basse-cour* or paved area where defenders could assemble out of sight before launching a sortie. Other defences were checked and where necessary replaced or strengthened, the chains and machinery on all gates being replaced in February 1419, and in 1425 a deep ditch or *fosse* was dug around Orléans. In 1427 the governor André Marchard was replaced by Raoul de Gaucourt, who made the last improvements before the siege began and, in September 1428, ordered a final count of available defenders.

Before the arrival of Jeanne d'Arc the morale of French armies seems to have depended on 'brotherhoods of arms' and various other forms of military association. These offered mutual support and helped pay or share ransoms. Networks of such associations developed, forming alliances or political factions. Jeanne's imposition of sterner morals on these armies largely seems to have been accepted by the common soldiers. She demanded a great deal – no swearing and the expulsion of all loose women, while everyone also had to attend Mass. The result was a startling increase in French morale which was soon reinforced by military success.

There is plenty of documentation concerning the numbers of French troops, but this tends to be conflicting and confusing. Some scholars estimate that during the siege the garrison of Orléans numbered from 1,600 to 2,400 professional soldiers and up to 3,000 local militia from a population of around 30,000. But in September 1428 an assessment by Hémon Raguier recorded only 740 men-at-arms and 870 crossbowmen in Orléans, Châteaudun and neighbouring Loire castles. The ordinary garrison of Orléans was probably around 400 but would soon have suffered casualties, perhaps falling to as little as 200 fit men before reinforcements arrived on 25 October 1428. The latter supposedly numbered 800 combatants according to the *Journal du Siège*. The money paid to five of their captains on 30 October refers to 219 men-at-arms plus 183 crossbowmen, and the forces of the other captains are likely to have been similar. According to records for December, 685 soldiers were being paid in Orléans, perhaps because the Scottish captain David Malleville had recently arrived with 60 men. But according to the

A mid-15th-century Flemish or French tapestry showing a small cannon or *culverin* with a fanciful dragon's head near the muzzle. It is being fired by a gunner who is either shielding his ear from the noise or is afraid that something will blow back into his face. The gun is also mounted in a wheeled carriage. (Musée du Château, Saumur; author's photograph)

Only the wealthiest leaders would have been able to afford this latest style of best quality armour. It is a superb 'white harness' or fully plated war armour made in Milan in the mid-15th century. (Historische Museum, Bern)

Journal du Siége, there were only 70 men-at-arms and 30 crossbowmen in Orléans in December. On 5 January 1429 the Admiral of France arrived, supposedly with 200 men. On the 24th La Hire arrived with 30 more, though these may merely have been returning. At the end of January Charles VII sent more reinforcements including the Scottish captains Patrick Ogilvy and John Stewart. In February 1429 the figures slumped though they returned to 58 men-at-arms and 27 crossbowmen in March 1429. These figures seem very small, but such professional soldiers were vitally important while urban militias played only a secondary role. Some sources hint that in March and April 1429, after a large part of the professional garrison had left, there were still around 2,000 assorted fighting men in Orléans – mostly ill-trained militia.

This process of gradual reinforcement and occasional withdrawal continued until the arrival of Jeanne d'Arc herself. The numbers may then have risen to 3,000, organised in about 60 companies, which meant that the defenders were now almost as numerous as the English besiegers. Yet it was not until June and July 1429 that the French achieved a significant numerical advantage over their enemies. Following the English abandonment of the siege, Arthur de Richemont arrived with an estimated 400 men-at-arms and 800 crossbowmen to help retake Beaugency, but even at this late date the figures did not necessarily reflect the troops available for a field army. The contrast with the numbers involved during earlier phases of the Hundred Years War is considerable, and even as recently as the battle of Vernieul in 1424 the French could field 10,000 men.

THE ENGLISH ARMY

There was no permanent English army at this time, merely some full-time constables, sergeants and other personnel who garrisoned royal castles. There were also up to 45 royal garrisons in France, each forming what was in effect a small standing army whose men were available to form a field army when needed.

Though the armies that served Henry VI and the Regent Bedford were generally known as 'The English', they included many Frenchmen plus mercenaries from various backgrounds. The Hundred Years War was, during this period, almost a civil war. Nevertheless, the so-called English armies did have the advantage of largely consisting of men from one realm – England – and being dominated by leaders of the same origin. Even so, English troops spoke dialects that must sometimes have been mutually incomprehensible. Not surprisingly most came from poor or geographically remote parts of the country, mostly from Yorkshire, Lancashire, Cumberland, Westmoreland, Cheshire, Somerset and Norfolk. The role of the upper aristocracy had declined in English military leadership, as it had in France, and only two field commanders in the Orléans campaign were senior noblemen, Salisbury and Suffolk. Many of the English professional captains were, in fact, only squires and came from similarly mixed or obscure social backgrounds as their French rivals.

England, unlike France, still raised soldiers by the well-established indenture system of fixed term, fixed conditions contracts. It would

Very little armour of ordinary 15th-century soldiers has survived and some that can be found in museums may be a mixture of real and fake pieces. This supposedly 15th-century infantry armour is an example. (Musées Royaux d'Art et d'Histoire, Brussels)

remain the basis of English enlistment for many years to come. In this indenture system, recognised military captains were told exactly the number and types of troops required, their wages, their length of service, methods of discipline and division of spoils. The archers largely consisted of longbowmen with only a small number of crossbowmen. The proportion of such archers to men-at-arms had also increased from the three archers to one man-at-arms preferred by Henry V, largely because archers were easier to recruit. Individuals often served more than once and many stayed on in France.

On 24 March 1428 a contract was agreed between Henry VI and the Earl of Salisbury. This, as usual, took the form of an *indenture of war* in which Salisbury agreed to serve in the King's wars in France, Normandy and other 'marches and frontiers' for six months starting on 30 June 1428. He would supply 600 men-at-arms and 1,800 archers levied solely in England, though Salisbury was permitted to replace 200 men-at-arms with three times as many archers. This Salisbury did and as a result he assembled 450 men-at-arms and 2,250 archers for service in France, largely engaged through Salisbury's own retainers and other dependants. These retainers included Salisbury's *hôtel*, meaning men who received a regular pension in his service. The army that assembled as a result in July 1428 consisted largely of volunteers engaged for this specific campaign; the contracts assuring these men that they could return to England at the end of their term of service. It is also worth noting that the force contained only one knight banneret and eight knights bachelor; the other men-at-arms not being of knightly status.

In Paris, Salisbury received royal letters which ordered him to raise another 400 men-at-arms and 1,200 archers in France, but in the event he could only find a further 200 men-at-arms and 600 archers or crossbowmen. Some were drawn from existing garrisons, though according to a record dated 1 February 1429, 12 garrisons in Normandy were only able to send 39 men-at-arms and 104 archers or crossbowmen to the siege of Orléans. Other French indenture contingents may have arrived earlier with Talbot and Scales. On 5 April 1429, the Grand Council of England would receive a desperate demand from the Regent Bedford for an additional 200 lances and 1,200 archers, but this was too late to alter the outcome of the campaign.

Theoretically Bedford should have been able to raise 1,400 men on a feudal basis for 26 days from those areas of France that recognised Henry VI. But absenteeism and the devastation of war meant that the number really available was negligible. Nevertheless, a summons was issued in November 1429 and repeated in April the following year. Bedford should similarly have been able to draw upon the militias of cities under his rule. Paris did send crossbowmen and other archers who took part in the Battle of the Herrings on 12 February 1429 but there were few other references to pro-English militia.

In some respects the troops involved on the English side were identical to those on the French side. This was certainly true of men-at-arms except that the English normally had only two horses instead of the French three. The big difference was, of course, amongst the archers. The great majority of those on the English side were longbowmen with relatively few crossbowmen whereas the opposite was the case in French armies.

In terms of gunpowder artillery the two sides were very similar, though during the siege of Orléans the English had slightly fewer and generally smaller guns than did the defenders. The English artillery of 1428–29 was, nevertheless, notably effective and had played a significant role in the conquest of Normandy. Cannon were no longer primitive, but it was changes in their support organisation that made the big difference, rather than improvements to the guns themselves. The men who organised the English artillery train were mostly specialists, retained and paid by the king, which enabled senior commanders to use guns to their full advantage. Such experts supervised materials for making guns, gunpowder and ammunition as well as traditional siege weapons. By the early 15th century, English 'Masters of the Ordnance' enjoyed considerable status and sometimes commanded artillery in the field. For example William Appleby, who was in charge of English artillery during the siege of Orléans, was to be treated 'like a mounted man-at-arms' in terms of dignity and rank. In addition to the 'Master of the Ordnance' himself, there were master cannoneers, varlets or apprentices, assorted assistants, carpenters, blacksmiths, other skilled workers and a French clerk-translator. Interestingly the known names of these men indicate that more of them were French than were English.

English commanders also enjoyed greater control over their troops than did their French opposite numbers. Men were fined for having insufficient or inferior equipment and were reviewed more or less regularly. Inspections were clearly carried out during the siege of Orléans. For example on 23 and 24 December 1428 two knights, Jean Popham and Jean de Handford, inspected the retainers of a squire named Thomas Giffard in one of the English siege positions. Forty-one men passed muster but for some reason two men did not, while seven others were absent with legitimate excuses. The same contingent was inspected a month later and again on 9 March 1429.

Foreign troops in this English army included men from Picardy, Champagne, Burgundy and other Burgundian territories. Some 1,500 Burgundian soldiers were, in fact, sent to help the English siege but were withdrawn in April 1429. It is again difficult to be specific about the number of troops involved. Estimates of the total at the start of the siege range from 2,500 to 4,000, but men would have been sent to garrison Châteauneuf, Jargeau, Meung and Beaugency. On 1 December Talbot and Scales arrived with 300 men, livestock and some cannon. One financial document states that there were around 800 men-at-arms and 4,250 archers paid at the end of the month but this probably excludes deserters, the injured, sick or recently killed, while probably including the newly arrived Burgundians. By 3 March 1429 the English government was spending 40,000 *livres tournois* a month on the siege, which corresponded to 1,333 men-at-arms and 4,000 archers, but in reality this sum would also have had to cover all other expenditures as well. On 11 April 1429, Bedford ordered continued payment for 950 lances and associated archers, totalling perhaps 3,800 men, though it is unlikely there were this many troops around Orléans. At end of the siege the English seem to have numbered nine knights banneret, 14 knights bacheler, two masters of artillery, 878 other men-at-arms, 2,596 archers, and 898 non-combatant pages, but not all necessarily present outside Orléans.

OPPOSING PLANS

THE FRENCH PLAN

The French plan was simple, though it became more ambitious as success fed upon success. If Orléans fell to the English, then Charles VII and his Armagnac supporters would almost certainly lose control of the Loire valley. So Orléans must not only be supplied with provisions and troops but the English siege must be broken. Since the English were operating at some distance from their primary base in Paris, their lines of communications were vulnerable, but the only major French attempt to intercept a large English supply convoy was defeated at the battle of the Herrings.

The revival of French morale which followed the arrival of Jeanne d'Arc led to a more determined attempt to reinforce Orléans. Once this was successfully achieved the defenders so damaged the besieging forces that the English commander abandoned his siege of Orléans altogether. Quite who was responsible for the way in which the French broke the siege is unknown. Jeanne d'Arc tends to get the credit but she had

RIGHT **The beautiful city of Chartres with its world-famous cathedral fell to the invading English before the siege of Orléans and then served as an assembly point for English armies operating in the Loire area. (author's photograph)**

LEFT **French manuscript of around 1415, illustrating troops attacking a fortified gate with a wooden** *barricade* **in front. Note the small cannon on a complicated frame in the lower corner of the picture. (***Chroniques de France***, British Library, Ms. Cotton Nero Ell, vol. 1, f.1, London)**

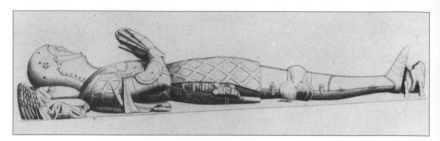

Effigy of John Fitzalan, Earl of Arundel in Arundel Church, made around 1435. Though this knight did not take part in the Orléans campaign, his armour covered by a tight-fitting *tabard* is typical of English equipment of the period. (ex-C.A. Stothard, *Monumental Effigies of Great Britain*, 1817)

wanted to attack the English immediately rather than simply to resupply the garrison. Nor did she select the English siege-work at Saint-Loup as the first target, though she was probably responsible for changing a diversionary raid into a full-scale attempt to destroy this English position. The English positions south of the river were the next targets as it was clear that these were the key to breaking the siege. Once again Jeanne d'Arc ensured that the French assaults maintained their momentum despite heavy casualties. What was, however, new was the degree of French commitment to the capture of such siege-works in the face of the large number of guns which they contained.

The timing of the subsequent French counter-offensive which retook the Loire castles reflected French concern about the approach of a large English relief army under the famous Fastolf, but whether the final French move in this campaign can really be called a 'plan' is a matter of debate. What the French commanders did was to seize an opportunity when it presented itself and, taking full advantage of their troops restored morale, immediately pursued the retreating English. Within a matter of hours they had inflicted a major battlefield defeat on their supposedly invincible foes. With the English field army destroyed and several of its senior commanders captured, the road to Reims and a proper coronation for King Charles VII lay open.

To describe this series of events in terms of a strategic plan is probably wrong. What the French commanders did with brilliant success was to take prompt advantage of rapidly changing circumstances. In doing so they showed themselves to be military leaders of the finest quality.

THE ENGLISH PLAN

The main difference between the English campaigns of the 14th century and those of the 15th century was that the former largely consisted of *chévauchées* or deep raids while the latter focused upon sieges. In the 14th century the English tried to undermine the French ability to resist by causing as much economic damage as possible. In the 15th century the English tried to take territory by the direct use of force. If the English had taken control of the middle Loire valley, they would have been in a position to strike directly at Charles VII's major centres of Bourges and Chinon. If these had been taken, then the English could realistically have hoped that France south of the Loire would fall to them, perhaps through a dual assault from the Loire and lands the English already held in south-western France.

At first the English hoped that Orléans would fall quickly, just as Jargeau, Châteauneuf, Meung and Beaugency had fallen. After the

A knight bids farewell to his lady and his son in an early 15th-century French manuscript. He wears the sort of armour that would have been seen in French armies during the relief of Orléans. (British Library Ms. Harl. 4431, f. 150, London)

death of the Earl of Salisbury and the spirited defence offered by the French garrison, English tactics changed. A prolonged blockade replaced a quick assault. In mid-winter the English strengthened this blockade, perhaps feeling confident that their troops now had adequate winter shelter while Charles VII's attempts to relieve Orléans had so far been somewhat feeble.

With the arrival of Jeanne d'Arc in the French camp, the initiative shifted to the French while the English did virtually nothing. With the collapse of the English siege of Orléans, however, the Duke of Bedford suddenly seems to have recognised the seriousness of the situation and gathered a powerful force to strengthen those Loire towns still in English hands. In the event this relief force arrived just too late to save Jargeau, Meung and Beaugency. Perhaps recognising that there was nothing left to be done, the English retreated towards Paris. What their experience did not teach them to expect was an immediate and well-organised French pursuit. The result was a catastrophic English defeat at Patay, where the previously almost invincible English field army was overwhelmed before it had time to establish the field-defences that had served it so well at Crécy, Poitiers, Agincourt and many other victories.

THE CAMPAIGN

Salisbury's army landed at Calais on 1 July after which he went to Paris to discuss the situation with Bedford and his Regency Council. The original plan had been to complete the conquest of Maine and Anjou, but by 1428 Charles VII seemed weaker than ever. So Bedford reluctantly agreed to a daring invasion of the central Loire valley with an attack on Orléans. One reason for Bedford's reluctance was the fact that Orléans belonged to Duc Charles d'Orléans, and to attack the lands of a man who was already a prisoner ran counter to the ethics of chivalry. Though Charles d'Orléans remained a prisoner of the English until 1440, his city was actually defended by a garrison loyal to Charles VII. The successful seizure of Orléans would also open the way for a campaign to finally defeat Charles VII.

Orléans commanded the crossing of the Loire which was closest to the Seine. Both rivers had been major arteries of communications since pre-Roman times and as a result Orléans had become one of the most important cities in France, strategically, economically, politically and culturally. Since 1344 it had been an *appanage* or fief of a series of royal princes and had become a major centre of the Armagnac faction. In the early 14th century Orléans had 12 quarters, plus several suburbs, but by the middle of the century the city's fortified wall had been extended to include the western suburb. The old western wall was demolished and, during the course of the 14th century, the new Porte Bannier took over from the Porte Parisie as Orléans' main exit towards Paris and Chartres.

Orléans' famous bridge was probably built in the 12th century. It had 20 arches with drawbridges at both ends. There were houses and shops on top and several watermills beneath. A small alluvial island had also emerged from the river beneath the northern half of the bridge during the 14th century. It consisted of two low mounds and here, in 1417, Étienne Gaudin and Étienne Paré, 'masters of the works of the Duke of Orléans', erected a small fortification or *bastille*. The much larger fortification of Les Tourelles at the southern end of the bridge might originally have been built in the 12th century, though the existing structure largely dated from the 14th and had been very recently strengthened. Shortly

The Cathedral of Ste. Croix in Orléans was rebuilt after being badly damaged by Protestants in 1567. King Henry IV, grateful that the city had supported him, undertook to reconstruct the building in pseudo-Gothic style. This work continued into the 19th century. (author's photograph)

BATTLE OF THE HERRINGS

1. English army under the Earl of Salisbury sails from Southampton to Harfleur and then marches to Paris (Summer 1428).
2. English army under the Earl of Salisbury marches from Paris to Chartres and establishes a forward base at Janville (August 1428). English then advance to the Loire river, constructing a defended position west of Orléans to protect the flank of an English siege-train as it passes close to the city (8 September) on its way to Meung. Meung surrenders the same day and the English move against Beaugency. Here the garrison resists in the castle and at the bridge so the English cross the Loire at Meung and attack Beaugency on 20 and 25 September. Beaugency surrenders (26 September). Smaller part of the English army moves along the southern side of the Loire to attack Jargeau on the south bank (falls 5 October), then crosses the Loire at Jargeau to attack Châteauneuf on the north bank (falls 6 October). English recross the Loire and advance to face French defences at the southern end of the bridge at Orléans (7 October). The main English force under Salisbury crosses south of the Loire at Meung and joins the smaller English force south of Orléans (12 October). English garrisons installed at Meung, Beaugency, Jargeau and Châteauneuf while the English gradually construct siege positions around Orléans. The blockade is never complete, particularly on the eastern side of the city.
3. The Bastard of Orléans (the future Dunois) makes unsuccessful sorties against the English around Orléans (30 December 1428 and 15 January 1429). Other sorties led by La Hire also fail to break the siege.
4. A large English supply column under Sir John Fastolf leaves Paris to support the besiegers around Orléans (February 1429).
5. Attempt to intercept the English supply column from Paris by a French force under the Comte de Clermont (A) from Blois (11 February 1429), to link up with a smaller French force from Orléans (B) under La Hire.
6. French find the English supply column near Rouvray but are defeated at the Battle of the Herrings (12 February 1429), so retreat back to Orléans.
7. Part of the now demoralised French army under the Comte de Clermont leaves Orléans and retreats to Tours.
8. Garrison of Châteaudun remains loyal to the Dauphin.

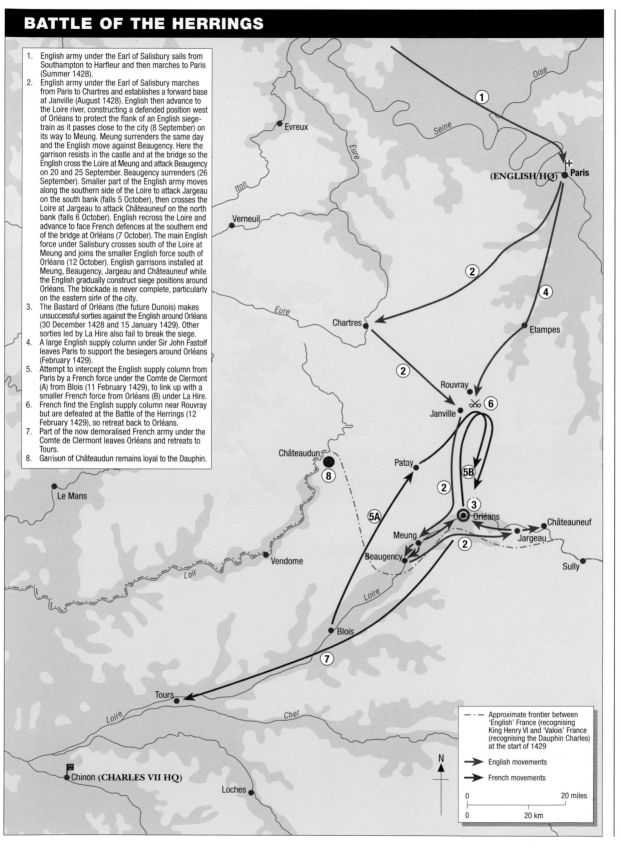

Approximate frontier between 'English' France (recognising King Henry VI and 'Valois' France (recognising the Dauphin Charles) at the start of 1429

English movements

French movements

0   20 miles
0   20 km

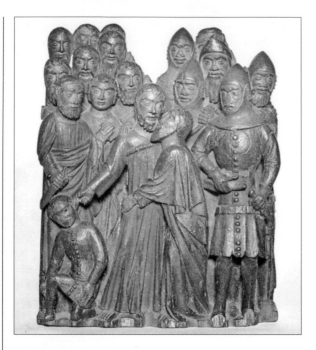

Several English works of art found their way to the Loire area, perhaps as a result of the English occupation of northern France. This painted wooden carving of 'The Arrest of Jesus' is one example dating from the early 15th century. (Musée des Arts Décoratifs du Château, Saumur)

before the English invaders arrived a small *boulevard* or field fortification was built on the river bank immediately in front of Les Tourelles. The city, along with several other fortified towns and castles including the almost isolated outpost of Châteaudun, were defended by garrisons under the command of Comte Jean de Dunois, better known as the Bastard of Orléans.

Meanwhile the English under the command of Salisbury advanced steadily towards Orléans. They left Paris in August 1428, assembled at Chartres then thrust forward to establish a defended base at Janville. On 8 September the English established some sort of position just west of Orléans to protect their flank as their siege train passed by on its way to attack Meung. This was probably at Saint-Laurent des Orgerily where they would later construct a major siege fortification. As yet Orléans itself was ignored. Meung surrendered the same day and the English pressed on to Beaugency, where a French garrison decided to defend only the castle and the bridge. Some of the English crossed over the Loire at Meung and attacked Beaugency from the southern bank on 20 and 25 September. Considering their position to be untenable, the French garrison surrendered on the 26th. Meanwhile Charles VII hurried reinforcements into Orléans and on the last day of September a large sum of money was distributed to French troops in Orléans and Chinon. As Enguerrand de Montstrelet made clear in his *Chronicles*, Orléans was not taken by surprise: *He* [the Earl of Salisbury] *came before it in the month of October, but as the garrison and inhabitants had long expected his arrival, they had provided themselves with all sorts of warlike stores and provisions, having determined to defend the place to the last extremity.*

Part of the interior and the exterior of a *brigandine*, a type of relatively light scale-lined armour used by men-at-arms and infantry during the 15th century. (Castle Museum, Warwick; author's photograph)

On 5 October an English force under Suffolk captured Jargeau east of Orléans, probably having arrived along the southern side of the river. The following day they crossed the Loire and took Châteauneuf on the north bank. Orléans now appeared to be isolated and on 7 October Suffolk made camp facing the French defences at the southern end of the bridge. Six days later the main English force under Salisbury joined him, whereupon the defenders of the city destroyed the Convent of the Augustins along with the surrounding suburb of Porteriau. But the French destruction of the Convent buildings was not complete and the English subsequently converted the ruins into a powerful *bastille* fortification.

THE SIEGE OF ORLÉANS BEGINS

This marked the official start of the siege of Orléans, though the English artillery bombardment does not seem to have begun until the 17th. One English gun called 'Passe-Voulant' shot stones weighting over ten kilos (22lb) which did considerable damage inside the city. On 21 October the English attacked Les Tourelles and its *boulevard* but this assault was driven off, the women of Orléans being credited with the French success because they constantly brought food, drink and supplies across the bridge. Also on the 21st Raoul de Gaucourt, governor of Orléans, fell off his horse and broke his arm, probably while organising the women volunteers carrying supplies to Les Tourelles. It was a fierce struggle, with the English losing an estimated 240 killed and the French around 200. Salisbury now changed his plan, abandoned the direct assault and sent pioneers to undermine the French *boulevard*. This was so successful that the defenders withdrew to Les Tourelles, but the English had so many cannon that Les Tourelles was now indefensible. So this bridge-fortress was also abandoned on the night of 23/24 October, the French breaking at least one arch of the bridge as they withdrew. The Earl of Salisbury was then killed by a remarkably accurate cannonball fired across the Loire from the Tour Notre-Dame on the very day he occupied Les Tourelles. Command of the English outside Orléans now passed to the more cautious Earl of Suffolk.

The Bridge over the Loire at Orléans during the siege of 1428–29, as seen from the west (after Alexandre Collin): A – The Châtelet citadel with its drawbridge; B – Watermills beneath three arches of the bridge north of the island of Saint-Antoine; C – The Hostel and Chapel of Saint-Antoine with the defensive Bastille of Saint-Antoine constructed between them; D – One arch of the bridge collapsed at an earlier date and was repaired with timber; E – Defensive Boulevard of La Belle-Croix built at the southern end of the French-held part of the bridge; F – One arch of the bridge destroyed by the French defenders; G – Two arches of the bridge destroyed by the English besiegers; H – Castle of Les Tourelles held by the English, with its drawbridge; I – Fortified Boulevard of Les Tourelles held by the English (probably of earth rather than stone as shown here); J – Ruined Church, Convent and Cloister of Les Augustins converted into a fortified *bastille*, held by the English.

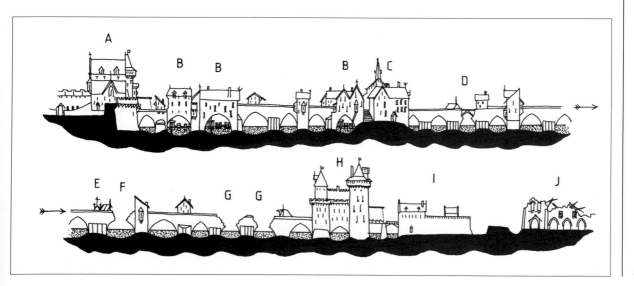

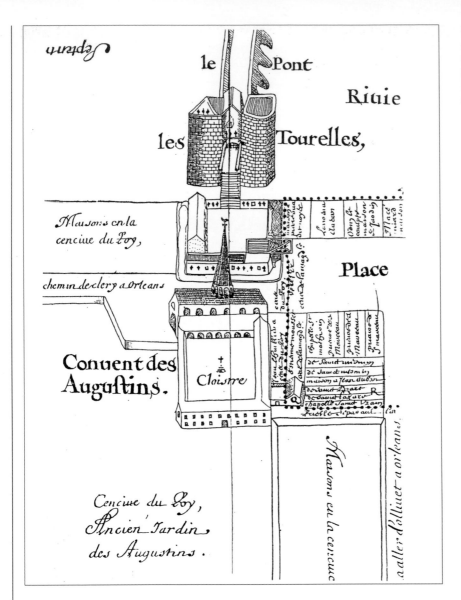

le Pont

Riuie

les Tourelles,

Septem

Maisons en la
cencive du Roy,

chemin de clery a Orleans

Place

Conuent des
Augustins.

Cloistre

Maisons en la cencive

a aller d'olliuet a orleans

Cencive du Roy,
Ancien Jardin
des Augustins.

The remaining bridge fortifications of Les Tourelles as they appeared in a plan drawn by Fleury in 1676. (Plan ZH35, Bibliothèque Municipale d'Orléans)

Having taken Les Tourelles, the English are said to have broken one or two further arches of the bridge. Some historians maintain that this would have been pointless for the English, but Suffolk now decided on a prolonged siege in which case defending the English position in Les Tourelles against French counter-attack would have made sense. On 24 October the English also constructed their first large siege-work, the Bastille des Augustins in the ruins of the Convent. A relatively ineffective blockade then continued until the end of November, but the city was so large that the English could not surround it. On 25 October Dunois returned with additional reinforcements. His route is unknown but was almost certainly from the south and then the east – essentially the same as that taken by Jeanne d'Arc many months later. Several senior French commanders accompanied Dunois, including Saint-Sévère the Marshal of France, Jean de Bueil, Jacques de Chabannes the Marshal of Bourbon, the Sire de Chaumont-sur-Loire Guillaume de Guitry, Théaulde de Valpergue the Lombard captain, Étiennes de Vignolles (La

DEFENCES OF ORLÉANS

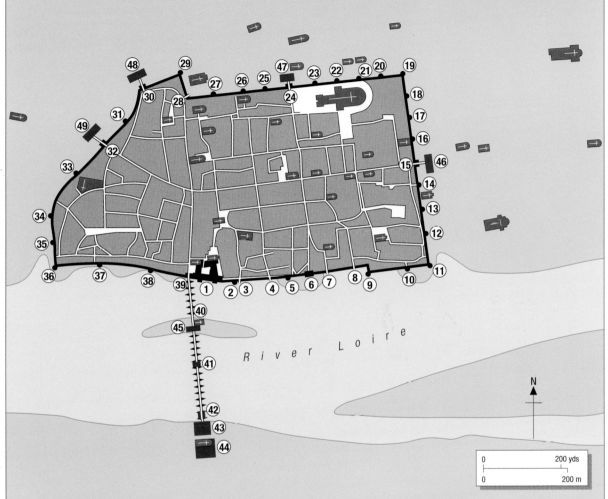

1. Citadel of Le Châtelet, with a large balista on its south-western tower to command the bridge.
2. Tower of the Feu Maître Pièrre le Queux.
3. Gate of the Lion d'Argent, leading to the river bank but walled up during the siege.
4. Gate of the Soleil, leading to the river bank but walled up during the siege.
5. Tower of the Croiche de Meffroy, with two large cannon on top during the early part of the siege though one was removed because it caused too much strain on the structure.
6. Postern Chesneau, the only postern remaining open to the River Loire during the siege.
7. Small gate of Saint-Benoît, leading to the river bank but walled up during the siege.
8. Small Gate of the Froidure, leading to the river bank but walled up during the siege.
9. Eight-sided Tour Carrée or Tower of Saint-Pierre-le-Puellier.
10. August Tower or Gate of the Tanners, leading to the river bank but walled up during the siege.
11. The New Tower, rebuilt as a small fortress with a moat in 1382; used as a major observation post during the siege, also with guns on top to bombard the English Boulevard Saint-Jean-le-Blanc and the English-held Les Tourelles fortress.
12. The White Tower.
13. Tower of Avalon.
14. Tower of Saint-Flou.
15. Gate of Burgundy or of Saint-Aignan with two flanking towers.

16. Tower of Saint-Étienne.
17. Tower of the Champ-Égron.
18. Tower of Aubilain or Aubelin.
19. Tower of the Falconry or of Mgr. l'Évêque; hoarding or upper wooden structure strengthened in 1403.
20. Tower of the Bishop's Plea.
21. Tower of the Church of Saint-Croix.
22. Unnamed tower.
23. Salty Tower.
24. Gate of Paris.
25. Tower of Jehan Thibaut.
26. Tower of Saint-Mesmin.
27. Tower of the Orchards of Saint-Samson; the cannon removed from the Tower of the Croiche de Meffroy placed on this tower during the last month of the siege.
28. Tower of Saint-Samson; used as an arsenal during the siege.
29. Tower of the Helmet; considered the second strongest part of the defences after the citadel of Le Châtelet.
30. Gate of the Banner.
31. Tower of the Feu Michau-Quanteau, built in 1404.
32. Gate of Renart.
33. Tower of the Eschifre de Saint-Paul; with siege engines on top during the siege.
34. Tower of André.
35. Unnamed tower.
36. Tower of the Barre Flambert or 'of the dock'; with a wall extended into the river to prevent a surprise attack along the river bank.

37. Tower of Notre-Dame; the cannon which killed the Earl of Salisbury at Les Tourelles on 24 October 1428 was fired from this tower.
38. Tower of the Gate of the Abreuvoir; leading to the river but walled up during the siege.
39. Two neighbouring Gates of the Portcullis and of the Bridge; the Gate of the Portcullis was a small postern allowing rainwater from the Rue des Hostelleries-Saint-Catherine to pour into the river; while the Gate of the Bridge gave access to the bridge over the Loire.
40. Mound and Chapel of Saint-Antoine; Hostel of Saint-Antoine or 'of the fishermen's mound' or 'of the broken barge'.
41. Defenders' Boulevard of La Belle-Croix on the French-held side of the broken bridge after the English captured Les Tourelles.
42. Fort of Les Tourelles and Boulevard of Les Tourelles on the broken end of the English-held side of the bridge.
43. Boulevard des Tourelles.
44. Boulevard des Augustins.
45. The French defenders' Bastille of Saint-Antoine constructed between the two Mounds (see 40).
46. Defensive boulevard constructed in front of the Gate of Burgundy.
47. Defensive boulevard constructed in front of the Gate of Paris.
48. Defensive boulevard constructed in front of the Gate of the Banner.
49. Defensive boulevard constructed in front of the Gate of Renart.

A detail from a French manuscript illustration of 'Alexander besieging Tyre'. Though slightly fanciful, the arms, armour and tents are realistic representations of mid-15th-century equipment. (*Histoire d'Alexandre*, Palais des Beaux-Arts de la Ville, Paris)

Hire) and an Aragonese named Sernay or Cernay who was Captain of the Vendôme. Five days later Dunois slipped out again by night, without interference from the English, and returned to Blois to confer with the Comte de Clermont, who was overall commander of the French army. The dense forests east of Orléans probably came closer to the city in the 15th century, and this would have helped screen French reinforcement and supply convoys in and out of Orléans.

The defenders of Orléans now began a methodical destruction of all the suburbs, including a large number of churches, in order to deny cover and winter shelter to the English besiegers. Charles VII had given Raoul de Gaucourt permission to take this drastic action back in April. On or by 8 November 13 churches had been burned and their walls pulled down. Other half-timbered buildings were simply burned to the ground. This was clearly a painful necessity for the citizens, as was recorded in the *Journal du Siège*. *And also they burned and demolished all the suburbs around the city, which were the most beautiful and rich to see before they were destroyed, because they had many large and rich buildings and they were said to be the most beautiful suburbs in the kingdom.* This destruction continued to 29 December, being recorded by almost all chroniclers. Enguerrand de Montstrelet also bemoaned that, *To prevent the Earl from fixing his quarters in the suburbs and fortifying them, the French had demolished the whole, including many excellent houses and upwards of twelve churches belonging to the four orders of mendicant friars, with several fine houses of recreation for the burghers of Orléans. By doing this they could discharge they cannon from the ramparts freely all around. Lord Salisbury,* [actually Suffolk by this time] *not withstanding this and in violent opposition from the garrison who made many sallies and fired on him from culverins and other instruments of death to the wounding and killing of many of his men, quartered himself and his army near to the walls.*

The construction of the English siege-works

Only after 8 November did the English move men to the north bank of the Loire to construct siege positions west and north of Orléans. As Enguerrand de Montstrelet again wrote, … *his men, in their usual manner, raised huts of earth to shelter themselves from the effects of the arrows which were showered at them from the battlements.* Thomas Basin wrote that these siege works were *constructed in the manner of châtelets* [small forts]. Other English commanders included Sir Lancelot de Lisle and Sir William Glasdale, whom the French records called 'Classedach'. The besiegers were, in fact, under the immediate command of Glasdale after Suffolk had apparently withdrawn from the front line.

The French defenders did what they could to interrupt this work but were as unsuccessful in this as the English were in isolating Orléans. For example on 30 November sorties were led by Marshal Saint-Sévère, La Hire, Poton de Xaintrailles, Jacques de Chabannes, Denis de Chailly and Cervay the Aragonese. On 1 December John Lord Talbot arrived and was probably made deputy commander with Lord Scales under the overall authority of Suffolk. Perhaps winter shelters had now been constructed. Certainly more troops turned up and the English siege became more active again.

On 7 December the English launched a tentative and unsuccessful attack across the broken Loire bridge against a fortification known as the Boulevard Saint-Croix, which the French had erected on their side of the broken arches. On 23 December a new and powerful French *bombard* started firing stone cannonballs weighing almost 12 kilos (26lbs) against Les Tourelles. The gun was mounted in the Tour Neuve and was directed by Guillaume Duisy, whom French chronicles described as a 'very subtle operator'. He was also in charge of two cannon named 'Rifflart' and 'Montargis' in another tower, while a fourth large cannon had been brought from Gien. On or by 29 December the garrison destroyed the remaining six churches outside the city walls and the following day Dunois led an unsuccessful sortie in an attempt to stop the English erecting further siege works. It was probably directed against the Bastille Saint-Laurent, which was constructed that day. This *bastille* was close to the north bank of the Loire and henceforth served as the English headquarters. The last day of 1428 also marked the beginning of a new phase in the siege, with English efforts now

'The Deposition', mid-15th-century Burgundian carving. The two soldiers on the right, one of whom has lost his head, again have typical equipment of the period. (State Hermitage Museum, St. Petersburg)

BELOW The seal of Jean, Duc d'Alençon. The iconography is traditional but the armour of course dates from the 15th century. (Archives Departmental de l'Orne, Alençon)

The effigy of Michael de la Pole, Earl of Suffolk, again provides an accurate and detailed representation of English knightly armour at the time of the Orléans campaign. This Michael de la Pole died at the siege of Harfleur in 1415 but one of his successors, William, 4th Earl of Suffolk, commanded the English throughout most of the siege. (ex-C.A. Stothard, *Monumental Effigies of Great Britain*, 1817)

focusing on the north side of the river. January 1429 saw several attempts to attack the western fortification of Orléans. On 2 January the English assaulted the Porte Renard but were driven back to the Bastille Saint-Laurent. The same day a convoy of food supplies including 400 sheep and 954 pigs entered Orléans.

Armed men and escorted convoys could clearly get in and out of the city but the ordinary citizens were trapped. Under such circumstances the ability to grow food within the walls must have become very important. Medieval cities like Orléans included gardens and vegetable patches but during a siege the growing of flowers would have been abandoned in favour of basic food crops. Only a generation earlier a remarkable treatise had been written by *The Goodman of Paris* to instruct his young wife in such skills. During the autumn, winter and early spring when the siege of Orléans actually took place, he offered the following advice: *Note that in rainy weather it is good to plant but not to sow, for the seed sticketh to the rake. In the season of All Saints* [1 November] *we have beans, but that they may not become frost-bitten, do you plant them towards Christmas and in January and February and at the beginning of March, and plant them thus at divers times so that if some be taken by the frost others be not … Spinach comes in February and has a long crenellated leaf like an oak leaf, and grows in tufts like greens and you must blanch them and cook them well afterwards. Beets come later.*

While the people of Orléans struggled to feed themselves, the siege continued outside their city walls. On 4 January the English again attacked the Porte Renard. On 5 January Louis de Culan the Admiral of France entered with reportedly 200 men. On the 6th the English erected the Boulevard de l'Ile Charlemagne on an island in the river and the Boulevard des Champs de Saint-Pryve on the south bank. These formed links between their existing positions at Les Tourelles and Saint-Laurent. The same day part of the garrison made another sortie led by Louis de Culan, Marshal Saint-Sévère and Théaulde de Valpergue. Some time during the first two weeks of January the English began extending their

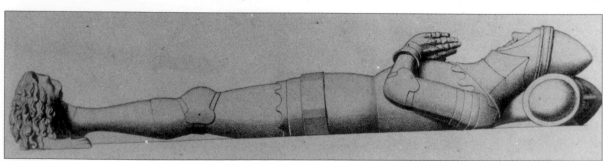

positions northwards by constructing the Boulevard de la Croix-Boisée. A sortie led by Dunois on 15 January may have been against this construction. On the 24th La Hire returned, though with only 30 men who were probably his own retinue. Two days later a more substantial force arrived under the command of the Scottish captain Patrick Ogilvy, Viscount d'Angers, and John Stewart, Lord Darnley, who was Constable of the Scottish army. On 27 and 29 January the English again attacked the Porte Renard with little result, while Raimon de Villars and the Xaintrailles brothers also entered Orléans on the 29th, bringing messages from Charles VII.

February began with similar small-scale skirmishing but would also see the biggest battle before the arrival of Jeanne d'Arc. On 4 February Charles VII authorised four captains to raise more troops to relieve Orléans. During the night of 5 February a small unit of 30 soldiers reached the city from Sologne. On the 8th William Stewart the brother of the Scottish Constable, plus Raoul de Gaucourt and the Sire de Verduzan, Jean Lescot, returned to Orléans. The same night 200 men under Guillaume Le Bret and 120 under La Hire also arrived. Clearly the French committed several of their most experienced leaders to this campaign, including Boussac the Lord d'Eu, the Bastard of Orleans, the Lords of Gaucourt, Graville and Vilain, Poton de Xaintrailles, La Hire, Théaulde de Valperghe and Louis de Vaucourt. To quote Enguerrand de Montstrelet: *They had under their daily command from twelve to fourteen hundred combatants, well tried and enterprising, but sometimes more and*

LEFT **The birthplace of Jeanne d'Arc in the village of Domrémy in eastern France. The little statue of the heroine in a niche above the door has 17th-century armour. (author's photograph)**

RIGHT **Several Spanish or Aragonese captains fought for Charles VII. Their men would have brought their own arms and armour, probably of the type shown in this Catalan panel-painting by Bernat Martorell made between 1425 and 1450. (Coll. Roig-Segimon, Barcelona)**

RIGHT **The poet Lydgate presents his book, 'The Pilgrim' to the Earl of Salisbury in a mid-15th-century English manuscript. The Earl was the son of the first English commander at the siege of Orléans. (British Library, Ms. Harl. 4826, London)**

ABOVE **This superb statue of Dunois, the Bastard of Orléans, was made after his death and portrays him in mid- or later 15th-century French armour with a wreath of victory around his head. (*in situ* Sainte-Chapelle, Château de Châteaudun; photograph Caisse Nationale des Monuments Historiques)**

sometimes less for the town was not so completely surrounded but that the besieged could replenish themselves with provisions or stores whenever they pleased. Very many sallies and skirmishes [were made] *… but from what I have heard from well informed persons, I do not find that the besieged did any great damage to the enemy except with their cannon and other like instruments from their walls. By one of these was slain Sir Lancelot de Lisle, a very valiant English knight and renowned in arms.*

Amongst the French gunners in Orléans was one of the best known of his day. This was Jean de Montesclerc, otherwise known as Master Jean of Lorraine, who had been recruited at Angers for a large sum of money on 1 February. He usually fired a gun in the Boulevard de la Belle Croix on the broken end of the bridge. There, according to the *Journal*, he would also tease the English: *To mock them he sometimes let himself fall to earth, feigning either death or wounds, and had himself carried into the town. But he would return quickly to the skirmish and did such so that the English would know that he was alive, to their great damage and displeasure.*

The Battle of the Herrings

Other French attempts to break the siege of Orléans were less successful. In February a large English supply column under Sir John Fastolf left Paris. Clearly Charles VII had agents in Paris because news of this convoy reached him almost immediately. On the 9th a number of

commanders slipped out of Orléans to confer with the Comte de Clermont, but this time they did not get through unmolested for the Bastard de Bourg was captured. Whether or not he was persuaded to tell the English of the French plans is unknown. The French had, in fact, decided to intercept Fastolf. As Clermont did not have enough troops to do this on his own, 200 men under Dunois left the city to join him at Blois on 10 February. The resulting French force may have numbered between 3,000 and 4,000 troops. Next day some other captains in Orléans, including Guillaume d'Albret, William Stewart, Saint-Sévère, both Xaintrailles brothers, La Hire and Verduzan also led their men to join Clermont's force as it intercepted the English supply column.

The result was the disastrous battle of Rouvray, otherwise known as the Battle of the Herrings because the English wagons were carrying so many barrels of salted fish. The French attacked across open country on 12 February but not before the English had time to draw up their supply wagons in a field fortification. Furthermore the French and their Scottish allies were fewer than the English had expected, so the latter counter-attacked from their wagons. Most of the Franco-Scots force had dismounted, contrary to orders, and were overwhelmed before they could retreat. The Scottish contingent was virtually wiped out. This defeat cost the French between 300 and 400 dead and had a shattering effect on their morale. On 18 February the Comte de Clermont abandoned Orléans and retreated to Tours, thus taking himself and his troops out of the campaign. Other leaders including La Hire fell back to Chinon, where Charles VII was so demoralised that he considered withdrawing to his own *appanage* of the Dauphiné in south-eastern France, or even abandoning France altogether.

Dunois remained in Orléans but argued against further sorties. For their part the citizens feared a surrender and begged the Duke of Burgundy to reach some arrangement with Bedford. The Duke was indeed uneasy about Bedford's attack on Orléans and seems to have withdrawn his Burgundian contingent from the siege. So the citizens of Orléans got Charles VII to allow them to send Poton de Xaintrailles and others to negotiate with the English in Paris. But Bedford's counsellors were confident the city would soon fall and maintained that England had spent too much money for the siege to be halted now, particularly if it would then be handed over to the Burgundians.

THE ARRIVAL OF JEANNE D'ARC

By March 1429 a large part of the garrison had left Orléans and the French position was beginning to look hopeless. Far away on the eastern

In addition to bridges over the Loire at Orléans and neighbouring towns, there were also several ferries and fords like the one used by Jeanne d'Arc at Checy. This example marked by rows of wooden piles is, however, on the outskirts of Orléans itself. (author's photograph)

1. Jeanne d'Arc journeys from Vaucouleurs to Chinon (23 February to 6 March 1429).
2. Jeanne d'Arc sent to Poitiers for interrogation by the French *parlement* in exile, then returned to Tours (March–April 1429).
3. Jeanne d'Arc goes from Tours to Blois (between 21 & 24 April 1429) where the Dauphin's army assembles, and is joined by the Bastard of Orléans and La Hire from Orléans.
4. Jeanne d'Arc and the French army move from Blois towards Orléans (26 April 1429), probably marching at some distance south of the English-held bridgeheads at Beaugency, Meung, Orléans and Jargeau. A large supply column with a relatively small covering force crosses the Loire by a ferry or ford at Checy (29 April 1429) while the bulk of the Dauphin's army remains south of the river.

— · — · — Approximate frontiers.
Note that there were several pro-Dauphin garrisons within nominally Burgundian and pro-King Henry VI territory.

0   50 miles

0   100 km

RIGHT **Sieges are often illustrated in 15th-century manuscripts, but carvings of the subject are much rarer. Here troops, probably representing Burgundians, place scaling ladders against a fortified wall while men-at-arms try to force the gate.** (*in situ* Hotel de Ville, Leuven; author's photograph)

OPPOSITE, TOP **The River Loire at Orléans is broad, shallow and has several large alluvial islands. Here is it seen from the south bank looking downstream from beneath the Pont George V.**

OPPOSITE, BOTTOM **Another view of the broad Loire from the same point looking upstream. The Cathedral rises in the distance while the tower of the Church of St. Donatien is closer to the riverbank. The medieval bridge crossed the Loire about 100 metres (109yds) from the Pont George V.** (author's photograph)

BELOW **A mounted dragon-slaying saint, probably St. George, appears in typical mid- to late-15th century armour on this carved English pew-end.** (*in situ* church, Hatch Beauchamp, Somerset; author's photograph)

frontier of France, however, something remarkable was happening. Here a young woman named Jeanne d'Arc had been 'hearing voices' since 1425. She was convinced that they came from Heaven via the Archangel Michael, Saint Margaret and Saint Catherine. These voices had told her to help chase the English from France and get Charles VII properly crowned at Reims. At first Jeanne argued with her voices, pointing out that she was not only a woman but was very young. But eventually, early in 1428, Jeanne d'Arc accepted that she had been given a Mission by God and so went to meet the pro-Valois military commander of Vaucouleurs, Robert de Baudricourt. Eventually she persuaded him to help her and, with the small escort that De Baudricourt provided, Jeanne d'Arc set out for Chinon on or around 23 February 1429. She travelled with two squires, Jean de Novellompont of Metz and Bertrand de Poulengy, plus Jean Colet de Vienne, who was one of King Charles's messengers. Each also had a valet. It was a dangerous journey, much of it through territory controlled by the Burgundian or pro-Lancastrian forces, until they reached land owing allegiance to Charles VII near the River Loire.

On 6 March Jeanne d'Arc reached Charles's headquarters at Chinon and was quickly sent to Poitiers for interrogation by the French *parlement* in exile, the Royal Council and a committee of theologians. These confirmed that Jeanne's religious faith was not heretical. Her virginity was also checked by senior ladies of the Court, including the Queen's mother, since it was believed that a woman who had dealings with the Devil could not be a virgin. Three weeks later Jeanne was returned to Tours.

Only now could her military ideas be taken seriously and, as Enguerrand de Montstrelet recorded: *Shortly afterwards orders were given to the marshal to take provisions and other necessities to Orléans, with a strong escorting force. Jeanne the Maid asked to go with him and to be given arms and armour, which was granted.* In addition to military equipment, Jeanne was allowed two young pages. One was Louis de Coutes, called Imerguet, who was described as a *good gentil homme who had exercised arms under Raoul de Gaucourt.* The other was a certain Raymond who was later killed in the unsuccessful attack on Paris. Five war horses and seven 'trotters' were allocated for Jeanne d'Arc's use while the banner she was given at Tours showed Christ between angels. Though it was in the shape of a military commander's pennon Jeanne was not yet given command of troops.

Between 21 and 24 April Jeanne d'Arc travelled to Blois, where Charles VII's army was assembling. There she was joined by Dunois and La Hire who had once again come from Orléans. The plan was for 400 to 500 troops to accompany another convoy of provisions into the besieged city. But this time the French mood seems to have

been changing, presumably as a result of Jeanne's presence. Several military leaders who had previously avoided getting involved in the Orléans campaign joined the force. Nor was there any attempt at secrecy, since Jeanne d'Arc sent a letter warning the English to abandon their siege. While Jeanne and the others were assembling at Blois, 100 other reinforcements led by Alain de Giron reached Orléans.

Despite the slump in morale which followed the Battle of the Herrings, things had not been entirely quiet around Orléans. On 10 March the English had erected yet another siege-fortification, the Bastille de Saint-Loup. This was the only position on the eastern side of the city and was obviously designed to cut the route into Orléans which had so often been used by reinforcements and supply convoys. It was, however, further from the walls than the other English positions and had no apparent effect on Orléans' communications with the outside world. On 16 March Sainte-Sévère left the city to take over the estates of his brother-in-law who had been killed at the Battle of the Herrings. Further reinforcements and money to pay the garrison entered the city, and the English also erected another siege-work, the Boulevard de la Grange-de-Cuiveret on 20 March. On 2 April there was a serious fight outside the Bastille Saint-Laurent during which both sides used cannon. Meanwhile the people of Orléans tried to repair their battered fortifications. On 8 April, for example, a mason named Imbert François was paid for four days work securing the ironwork of the Porte Bannier and repairing Tour du Heaume.

A flurry of English building activity now suggested that the besiegers knew an attempt would soon be made to relieve the city, though they were uncertain which direction it would take. On 9 April they erected

The Croix de la Pucelle and the little square on the site of the medieval Convent of the Augustinians on a particularly rainy day. The trees are on an island in the Loire and the city of Orléans rises through the mist beyond. (author's photograph)

the Boulevard de la Pressoir-Ars, followed by the Bastille Saint Pouair on the 15th and the Bastille de Saint-Jean-le-Blanc on the 20th. On 24 April the French garrison received 40 reinforcements led by Bourc the Bastard de Mascaran, followed three days later by 60 troops from the nearby town of Beaune la-Rolande en Beauce. On 28 April a famous captain, Florent d'Illiers the brother of La Hire, supposedly arrived with no less than 400 men from Châteaudun though this number is probably exaggerated. Then, early on the 29th, the same day that Jeanne d'Arc would arrive, 50 infantrymen appeared from the Gâtinais area north-east of Orléans.

Jeanne d'Arc's own march from Blois to Orléans has been clouded in pious legend. She and the supply column left Blois on 26th April, preceded by a large number of priests who sang the *Veni Creator Spiritus* but who returned to Blois two nights later. The precise route is unknown but must have been the same as that used by the others who had travelled between Blois and Orléans since the siege began. Jeanne and her companions reached the Loire at a ford or ferry near Checy. Why this was unguarded by the English is unknown. Perhaps it lacked sufficient boats to be considered important, or perhaps it was held by French troops from Orléans.

Written sources then mention a 'miraculous' change in wind direction and a sudden rise in the river's water level which enabled the supply convoy to cross the Loire with ease. Reading between the lines this suggests that boats or barges from Orléans were able to sail upriver, perhaps avoiding interference from the Boulevard Saint-Loup by going south of the Ile Saint-Loup through a shallow channel, then arriving at Checy, where they helped take the troops and the supplies to the north bank. Whether some or all of the escort then returned to Blois, or took up position south of Orléans to keep an eye on the English is again unclear. What is known is that Jeanne d'Arc entered Orléans around 8 o'clock in the evening of 29 April 1429 with some 200 men-at-arms accompanied by Dunois and other captains.

Jeanne urges Glasdale to abandon the siege

The final phase in the siege of Orléans had now been reached. Next day, 30 April, La Hire led the Orléans militia in a sortie against the Boulevard de Saint-Pouair. Meanwhile Jeanne d'Arc went to the end of the broken Loire bridge and urged Sir William Glasdale in Les Tourelles to abandon the siege. The English reaction was distinctly negative, as later described in Jeanne's rehabilitation trial: *A certain man named the Bastard of Granville* [actually Glasdale] *spoke many insults to Jeanne, asking her if she wished them to surrender to a women, and calling the French with her unbelievin pimps.* The *Journal* confirmed the evening conversation: *But Glasdale ar those on his side responded evilly, insulting her and calling her cow-girl … cryi very loudly that they would burn her if they captured her.* Jeanne also s herals to the English demanding that an earlier messenger be released. If the English would not release this messenger, Jeanne threatened to kill all the English prisoners in Orléans including those lords held for ransom. The French herald was released.

On 1 May money, perhaps brought from Blois by the supply column, was paid to the captains in Orléans who then paid their men. Jeanne and her companions rode around the streets, encouraging the people and having an immediate impact on morale in the city. Dunois, however, considered that more men were needed before the siege could be raised, and so returned to Blois to fetch them while La Hire seems to have been left in military command of Orléans. On 2 May, another quiet day, Jeanne d'Arc and her companions rode outside the city walls to assess the English strength. Jeanne apparently concluded they were weaker than had been thought. The following day, the last of these quiet days, saw religious processions within the city and the probable arrival of some more reinforcements.

The French capture the Boulevard Saint-Loup

On 4 May Dunois returned with additional troops. La Hire rode out to meet him or to ensure there was no interference from the Boulevard Saint-Loup, though the precise sequence of events has again be clouded by pious legend. There was clearly an attack on the Boulevard Saint-Loup and this appears to have started before Jeanne d'Arc knew about it. It may have been a diversion to allow Dunois's convoy a clear passage. Jeanne then galloped out to take part, perhaps at the head of a large band of volunteers. The fight developed into a serious assault on the English siege position by 1,500 men.

John Lord Talbot was informed of the situation and set out around the northern perimeter of the English lines to mount a diversionary attack from the Bastille Saint-Pouair. But he was himself diverted by a French sortie from the Porte Parisie by 600 men under Sainte-Sévère, Graville, Coulonces and others. When volumes of smoke were seen to the east it became obvious that Saint-Loup had fallen and was being destroyed by the French, so Talbot called off his own attack. The Chronicles of Enguerrand de Montstrelet described the fight: *Jeanne the Maid rose early and spoke to several captains and other men-at-arms, pursuading them in the end to arm and follow her because she wanted, as she put it, to get at the enemy, adding that she knew they would be defeated. The captains and soldiers were amazed at what she said, but they nevertheless armed and went with her to that part of the English fortifications known as the Bastille Saint-Loup, which was particularly strong. It was held by three or four hundred English but they were soon beaten and all of them either killed or wounded or captured, and the tower demolished and burned. Then the Maid returned to Orléans with all the knights and men she had led, and there she was feasted and acclaimed with joy by all ranks of men.*

OVERLEAF
THE FRENCH ARMY'S 'MIRACULOUS' CROSSING OF THE LOIRE AT CHECY, 29 APRIL 1429
The French advance-guard and supply train reached the Loire to find that the water was too low for the ferry to operate, while the wind was also blowing in the wrong direction. But when Jeanne d'Arc herself arrived the water rose and the wind changed. As a result the supplies and sufficient troops to protect them were taken across the Loire with ease. This not only raised the morale of Charles VII's army but came to be seen as miraculous, adding greatly to Jeanne d'Arc's credibility. (Graham Turner)

Men, including archers, men-at-arms, gunners and priests attack the Citadel of Women in a Flemish manuscript illustration in 1442–43. (*Champion des Dames* by Martin le Franc, Bib. Royale, Ms. 9466, f.4r, Brussels)

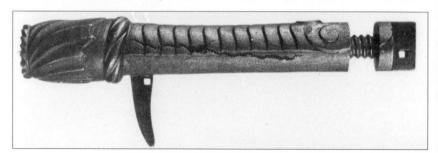

Dunois had not wanted a major attack, perhaps fearing that failure would destroy the newly revived but still fragile French morale, but the success at Saint-Loup confirmed the defenders of Orléans in their new-found confidence. Around 140 English had been killed and 40 prisoners had been taken. On 5 May Jeanne d'Arc sent another letter to the English in Les Tourelles, attached to an arrow shot from the broken bridge. In it she promised to release some of the prisoners taken at Saint-Loup if another of her detained messengers was set free. In reply the English shouted back that she was 'the whore of the Armagnacs', which apparently made Jeanne cry.

The French now had two tactical choices. They could attack the lightly defended enemy positions on the north bank or go for the strong English positions at Les Tourelles which would have to be attacked eventually. The latter course was chosen and on 5 May the French moved against the small Boulevard de Saint-Jean-le-Blanc east of Les Tourelles. Troops were ferried to the Ile aux Toiles, where two boats were commandeered to make a floating bridge across a narrow channel to the south bank. The English, however, abandoned the Boulevard de Saint-Jean-le-Blanc before the French arrived, falling back to the Bastille des Augustins and Les Tourelles.

The struggle had now reached a crisis. News of a large English relief army from Paris, led by the redoubtable Fastolf, had reached Orléans, though in fact Fastolf would not leave Paris for another month. There was also fear of dissension between the French leaders. Jeanne d'Arc and Dunois were already in disagreement on tactical matters, with Raoul de Gaucourt supporting Dunois and an increasing proportion of the ordinary soldiers agreeing with Jeanne.

THE STORMING OF LES TOURELLES

On 6 May a large numbers of soldiers and militia assembled inside the eastern gate of Orléans where Raoul de Gaucourt had been ordered to stop unauthorised sorties. He tried to stop the excited horde leaving but when Jeanne d'Arc accused him of being a 'bad man' some soldiers started to shout 'Death to Gaucourt!' The old man gave way and the troops streamed out, formed up near the Porte de Bourgogne and then made their way across the river towards the English positions. Recognising the inevitable, and obviously hoping to regain control of events, Dunois and the other senior captains joined them. To quote the *Journal du Siège: The English sallied out of the Tourelles in great strength, shouting loudly, and made a charge against them which was very strong and harsh. But the Maid and La Hire, and all of their army, joined together and attacked the English with such great force and courage that they caused them to recoil all the way back to their boulevard and the Tourelles.* It is a tribute to Raoul de Gaucourt's reliability in the eyes of established commanders that he was sent to guard the floating bridge during the English counter-attack, in case the French had to retreat. The Bastille des Augustins was quickly overrun and many French prisoners were freed.

During this fighting, notable feats of arms were reported on both sides. At Jeanne d'Arc's rehabilitation trial, her squire, Jean d'Aulon, recalled how a man-at-arms from Spain named Alfonso de Partada and another un-named man-at-arms raced each other towards the enemy. They were then stopped by a very large and well-armed Englishman, so Jean d'Aulon called the famous gunner Master Jean le Cannonier from Lorraine to shoot down the Englishman, which he did. The two competing men-at-arms and their followers then entered a breach and captured the *bastille*, whereupon the surviving English fled into the *boulevard* in front of Les Tourelles. This the English had strengthened since they took it back in 1428.

Dunois and the other leaders wanted their men to rest, but Jeanne d'Arc demanded an immediate assault before the English could strengthen their position even further. In fact Jeanne was excluded from a council of war that evening. When she heard of this she sent her confessor, Friar Jean Pasquerel, to tell the troops to get up early and be ready to attack next morning. Clearly Jeanne wanted to maintain their enthusiasm. Meanwhile English troops in the other siege positions made no attempt to come to the aid of Les Tourelles.

The enthusiasm of the ordinary people of Orléans in supporting the combatants is reflected in the *Journal*; [they] *were most diligent throughout the night in carrying bread, wine and other victuals to the men of war carrying on the siege.* Jeanne herself rose early on the 7th, confessed and heard mass as usual, then roused the troops. There is no evidence of any special speeches. Instead Jeanne d'Arc merely told the soldiers that although many of them would die they would go straight to heaven. The defences which now faced them

The Tour Neuve is the only surviving tower from the 15th-century fortifications of Orléans. It was a vital element in the defences at the south-eastern corner of the city. (author's photograph)

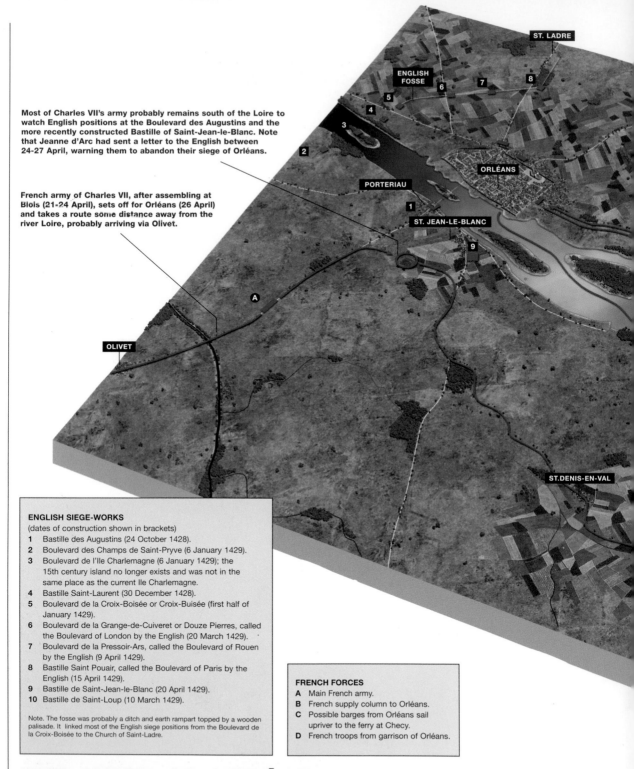

Most of Charles VII's army probably remains south of the Loire to watch English positions at the Boulevard des Augustins and the more recently constructed Bastille of Saint-Jean-le-Blanc. Note that Jeanne d'Arc had sent a letter to the English between 24-27 April, warning them to abandon their siege of Orléans.

French army of Charles VII, after assembling at Blois (21-24 April), sets off for Orléans (26 April) and takes a route some distance away from the river Loire, probably arriving via Olivet.

ENGLISH SIEGE-WORKS
(dates of construction shown in brackets)

1   Bastille des Augustins (24 October 1428).
2   Boulevard des Champs de Saint-Pryve (6 January 1429).
3   Boulevard de l'Ile Charlemagne (6 January 1429); the 15th century island no longer exists and was not in the same place as the current Ile Charlemagne.
4   Bastille Saint-Laurent (30 December 1428).
5   Boulevard de la Croix-Boisée or Croix-Buisée (first half of January 1429).
6   Boulevard de la Grange-de-Cuiveret or Douze Pierres, called the Boulevard of London by the English (20 March 1429).
7   Boulevard de la Pressoir-Ars, called the Boulevard of Rouen by the English (9 April 1429).
8   Bastille Saint Pouair, called the Boulevard of Paris by the English (15 April 1429).
9   Bastille de Saint-Jean-le-Blanc (20 April 1429).
10 Bastille de Saint-Loup (10 March 1429).

Note. The fosse was probably a ditch and earth rampart topped by a wooden palisade. It linked most of the English siege positions from the Boulevard de la Croix-Boisée to the Church of Saint-Ladre.

FRENCH FORCES
A   Main French army.
B   French supply column to Orléans.
C   Possible barges from Orléans sail upriver to the ferry at Checy.
D   French troops from garrison of Orléans.

THE SIEGE OF ORLÉANS

29 April 1429, viewed from the south-west showing the French army's march from Blois, keeping well south the river. While the main force probably remains south of the bridge over the Loire, the supply column that Jeanne d'Arc is accompanying crosses the river and enters Orléans from the east.

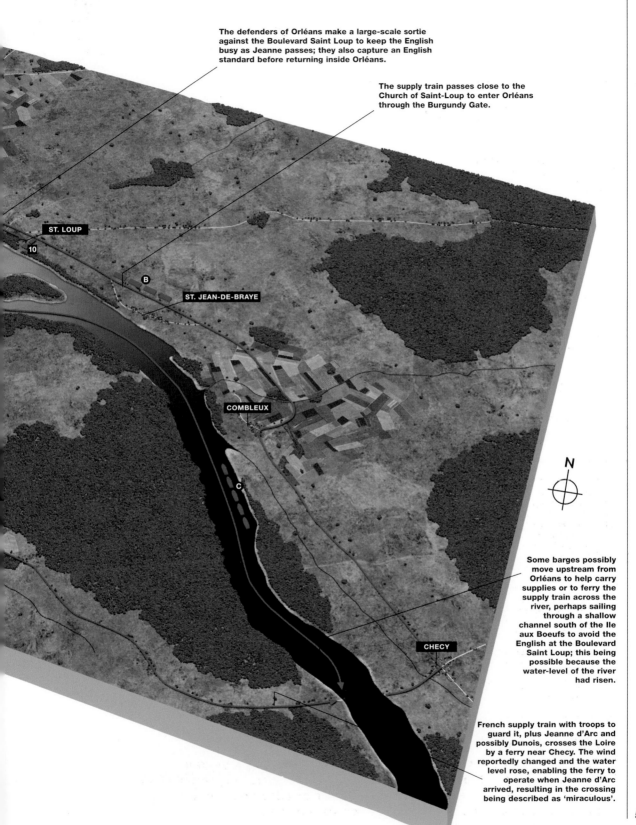

The defenders of Orléans make a large-scale sortie against the Boulevard Saint Loup to keep the English busy as Jeanne passes; they also capture an English standard before returning inside Orléans.

The supply train passes close to the Church of Saint-Loup to enter Orléans through the Burgundy Gate.

ST. LOUP

10

B

ST. JEAN-DE-BRAYE

COMBLEUX

C

N

Some barges possibly move upstream from Orléans to help carry supplies or to ferry the supply train across the river, perhaps sailing through a shallow channel south of the Ile aux Boeufs to avoid the English at the Boulevard Saint Loup; this being possible because the water-level of the river had risen.

CHECY

French supply train with troops to guard it, plus Jeanne d'Arc and possibly Dunois, crosses the Loire by a ferry near Checy. The wind reportedly changed and the water level rose, enabling the ferry to operate when Jeanne d'Arc arrived, resulting in the crossing being described as 'miraculous'.

ABOVE **The Church of St. Aignan, patron saint of Orléans, stood just outside the eastern wall of the medieval city. It was virtually destroyed by the defenders during the siege to deny shelter to the English, but was rebuilt soon afterwards, being re-consecrated in 1509. (author's photograph)**

appeared impregnable, being both high and strong. They were defended by between 700 and 800 English troops, according to French estimates but, undaunted by the presence of large numbers of English cannon, Jeanne personally led the attack.

The result was the bloodiest engagement since the battle of Agincourt. The French tried to scale the walls of the *boulevard*, particularly 'at the angles' but the English resisted strongly and there were heavy casualties on both sides. Jeanne herself was wounded by an arrow which, according to Dunois; 'pierced her flesh between her neck and her shoulder for a depth of half a foot'. It was shot from a high angle and penetrated a joint in her plate armour. Nevertheless, Jeanne continued fighting. Nor would she take medication or uses 'charms' which she regarded as akin to black magic. Only later did Jeanne d'Arc, frightened and weeping according to her confessor, agree to have her wound cleaned with olive oil. By 8.00pm the French were still not making progress and their leaders were getting disheartened. Dunois suggested drawing back into the city but Jeanne asked for more time. She mounted her horse and went to pray in a nearby vineyard. Seven minutes later, according to Dunois: *She returned from that place, immediately took her standard in her hand, and placed it on the side of the ditch. Instantly, once she was there, the English became afraid and trembled. The soldiers of the king regained their courage and began to climb up, making an attack on those inside the boulevard and not finding any resistance.*

Again Jeanne's young squire, Jean d'Aulon, recalled specific episodes. Towards the end of the day when the French had been forced to pull back, Jeanne's standard bearer was exhausted and gave the flag to a follower of the Lord of Villar named 'the Basque'. D'Aulon feared that the men would panic if they saw the banner being withdrawn so he asked 'the Basque' if he would follow if D'Aulon went to the foot of the *boulevard*. The Basque agreed, so D'Aulon went down into the ditch

OVERLEAF
**SIR WILLIAM GLASDALE INSULTS
JEANNE D'ARC ACROSS THE
BROKEN BRIDGE, 30 APRIL 1429**
Quite what Jeanne d'Arc hoped
to achieve by her conversation
with Sir William Glasdale, the
current commander of the
English forces, is unclear.
Perhaps she really did believe
that she had to let the enemy
know that her cause was blessed
by God. Or perhaps she was
trying to get the English to come
out of their fortified *boulevards*
and attack Orléans. Glasdale's
response to Jeanne's call was
insulting and obscene, but
otherwise the English did not
take the bait. (Graham Turner)

RIGHT **'King Philippe Augustus
captures Le Mans', in a French
manuscript illustration of around
1420. This manuscript provides
perhaps the best pictures of
French military equipment during
the period of the siege of
Orléans. (***Les Grandes
Chroniques de France***, Bib.
Municipale, Ms. 512, Toulouse)**

LEFT **The centre of Orléans is
surrounded by broad avenues
which run from the modern Pont
Marshal Joffre to the railway
bridge. The western and
northern avenues mark the line
of the English siege positions,
though no trace of the latter now
exist. The end of the English line,
except for the isolated Bastille
Saint-Loup east of the city, was
at a *bastille* between Saint-
Pouair and Saint-Ladre, known to
the English as the Bastille of
Paris. It stood approximately
where a tower-block can be seen
in this photograph. The large
church on the left is that of
St. Paterne, known during the
Middle Ages as Saint-Pouair.
It was demolished during the
siege and rebuilt afterwards.
(author's photograph)**

while covering himself with his shield. He had expected his companions
and 'the Basque' to follow but they held back. When Jeanne noticed her
banner in the hands of a stranger she thought it had been captured and
so snatched it from 'the Basque'. D'Aulon saw what was going on and
accused 'the Basque' of breaking his promise. Ashamed at this
accusation 'the Basque' grabbed back the banner and ran with it to
D'Aulon. This seems to have encouraged the men who, seeing Jeanne's
banner rush forward, themselves streamed forward and overran the
English *boulevard*.

The *Chronicles* of the Burgundian Enguerrand de Montstrelet provide
an objective account of the capture: *On Saturday they made a determined and
courageous attack on the strongly fortified tower at the other end of the bridge. This
tower was of very solid construction and defended by the flower of England's most
experienced men-at-arms. For a long time they held their own with skill, but to no
avail, for they were finally defeated by the sheer strength and courage of the attack,
and the greater part were put to the sword. Among these was a brave and renowned
English captain known as Glasdale, and with him was the Seigneur de Moulins, the
Bailiff of Evreux and several other rich noblemen of great importance.*

Jeanne d'Arc called upon Glasdale to surrender but again he would not. Instead Glasdale tried to lead his men back into the fortress of Les Tourelles but the drawbridge collapsed. Many fell into the river including Sir William De Moleyns and Glasdale who, being fully armoured, were drowned. Glasdale is said to have been clutching the banner of the Black Prince's great captain Chandos when he fell. The collapse of the drawbridge probably resulted from damage caused by a fire-ship which had been driven beneath it. Apparently some Orléans boatmen took a barge, made it into a fire-ship and jammed it somewhere beneath Les Tourelles. Placing it below the wooden drawbridge would have made more sense than driving it beneath the stone tower itself. Clearly morale inside Les Tourelles now collapsed and the surviving English garrison surrendered.

Enguerrand de Montstrelet was eager to ensure that not all the credit went to Jeanne d'Arc. *In these three assaults is was commonly held that the Maid Jeanne had been leader, but it must not be forgotten that she had with her all or most of the noble knights and captains who had been in the city throughout the siege ... They had all conducted themselves with such exemplary courage as is expected of men-at-arms that in these three battles between six and eight thousand of the enemy were killed* [clearly a great exaggeration] *while the French lost only one hundred men of all ranks* [almost certainly an under-estimate]. It has also been suggested that the Orléans militia made timber repairs to the broken bridge arches, thus threatening Les Tourelles from both sides. The bridge was in fact open during the night of 7/8 May, enabling Jeanne d'Arc and other wounded soldiers to be taken into the city for treatment.

Most medieval effigies of the aristocracy were destroyed during the French Revolution, but drawings of many of the finest were made before they were lost. This was the effigy of Guillaume, the early 15th-century Châtelain of Beauvais, and his wife Jeanne de Coudon. The Châtelain wears typical French armour of the period. (ex-Gaignieres)

THE ENGLISH ABANDON THE SIEGE

The following day, 8 May, the English abandoned their remaining siege positions, but instead of immediately withdrawing from Orléans they formed up in two large bodies between their siege-lines and the walls of the city. Quite why this was done is unknown. It may simply have been a defiant gesture, or to ensure that the French did not attack as the English withdrew, or perhaps the English genuinely hoped that the French would accept a challenge to battle. The French did form up facing their enemies outside the walls, but Jeanne d'Arc and probably the other professional commanders ordered their men not to attack. This stalemate lasted until the English turned and marched away. One group under Talbot and Scales retreated towards Meung while the other under Suffolk marched to Jargeau. Some French troops then disobeyed orders and attacked the retreating English, capturing cannon and other weapons. The siege of Orléans was ended. It had lasted 210 days.

Medieval France had huge areas of forest but, unlike England, many of these still exist. The English relief and supply columns that went from Paris to Orléans passed through several of them, the first being the Forest of Fontainebleu south of the French capital seen here. Meanwhile the Forest of Orléans north and east of that city probably gave cover to French forces entering and leaving Orléans during the siege of 1428–29. (author's photograph)

The day the English left a further payment was given to the troops in Orléans. According to the *Chronicles* of Enguerrand de Montstrelet: *There was great rejoicing throughout the city of Orléans … for they were now delivered from their treacherous enemies who had kept them for so long in great danger, and could see the survivors marching away to make their peace with God. A number of experienced men-at-arms were dispatched to examine the towers and fortifications. Here they found provisions and considerable supplies of various kinds, which they brought back to the town and with which they prepared a feast all the more enjoyable in that it had cost them nothing.* According to some French sources, Glasdale's body was also retrieved, cut up and embalmed so that it could be sent back to England.

Scales and Talbot now took command of the main English force at Meung with Matthew Gough in command of the Beaugency garrison. Talbot then returned to Paris at some unknown date, perhaps to warn Bedford that the English were in danger of losing their positions along the Loire and in the Beauce region if not reinforced. According to Enguerrand de Montstrelet: *The Duke of Bedford was greatly depressed at the news, but seeing that he had to do something he hastily collected men of various nations under his control, and sent about four or five thousand of them to the Orléanais under the command of Sir Thomas Rampstone and the Bastard of Thian, amongst others. He sent a promise that he would himself follow shortly afterwards with the reinforcements he had requested from England.*

On the French side the leaders in Orléans asked Charles VII to come and lead their troops, but instead the King sent several senior captains

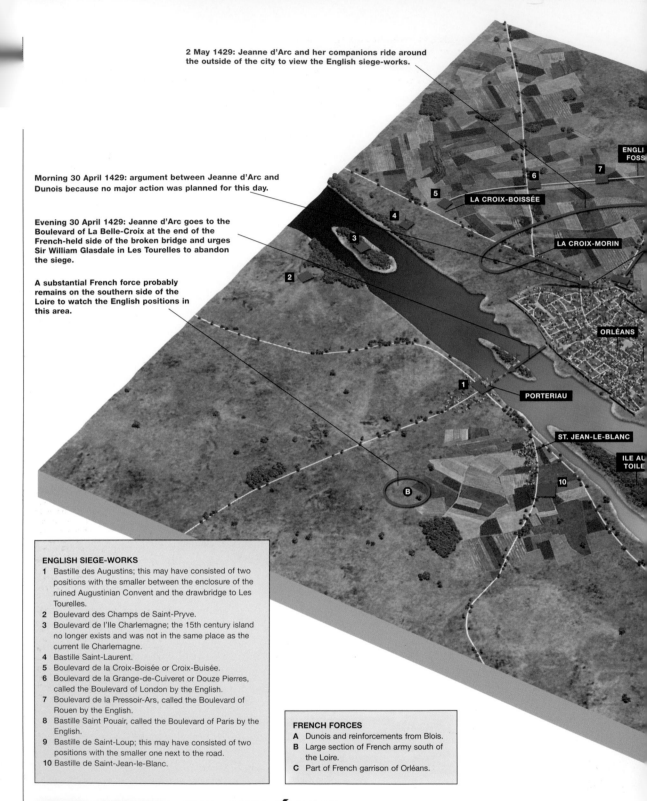

2 May 1429: Jeanne d'Arc and her companions ride around the outside of the city to view the English siege-works.

Morning 30 April 1429: argument between Jeanne d'Arc and Dunois because no major action was planned for this day.

Evening 30 April 1429: Jeanne d'Arc goes to the Boulevard of La Belle-Croix at the end of the French-held side of the broken bridge and urges Sir William Glasdale in Les Tourelles to abandon the siege.

A substantial French force probably remains on the southern side of the Loire to watch the English positions in this area.

ENGLISH FOSS

LA CROIX-BOISSÉE

LA CROIX-MORIN

ORLÉANS

PORTERIAU

ST. JEAN-LE-BLANC

ILE AU TOILE

ENGLISH SIEGE-WORKS

1 Bastille des Augustins; this may have consisted of two positions with the smaller between the enclosure of the ruined Augustinian Convent and the drawbridge to Les Tourelles.
2 Boulevard des Champs de Saint-Pryve.
3 Boulevard de l'Ile Charlemagne; the 15th century island no longer exists and was not in the same place as the current Ile Charlemagne.
4 Bastille Saint-Laurent.
5 Boulevard de la Croix-Boisée or Croix-Buisée.
6 Boulevard de la Grange-de-Cuiveret or Douze Pierres, called the Boulevard of London by the English.
7 Boulevard de la Pressoir-Ars, called the Boulevard of Rouen by the English.
8 Bastille Saint Pouair, called the Boulevard of Paris by the English.
9 Bastille de Saint-Loup; this may have consisted of two positions with the smaller one next to the road.
10 Bastille de Saint-Jean-le-Blanc.

FRENCH FORCES

A Dunois and reinforcements from Blois.
B Large section of French army south of the Loire.
C Part of French garrison of Orléans.

THE SIEGE OF ORLÉANS

30 April–4 May 1429, viewed from the south-west. Dunois travels back to Blois to collect additional troops. On his return the defenders seized the isolated English siege-position at Saint-Loup.

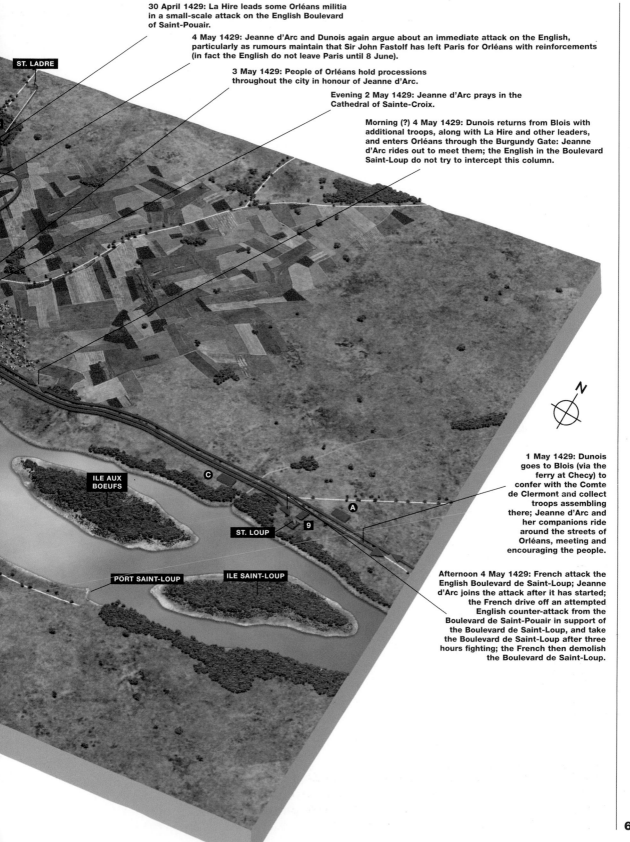

30 April 1429: La Hire leads some Orléans militia in a small-scale attack on the English Boulevard of Saint-Pouair.

4 May 1429: Jeanne d'Arc and Dunois again argue about an immediate attack on the English, particularly as rumours maintain that Sir John Fastolf has left Paris for Orléans with reinforcements (in fact the English do not leave Paris until 8 June).

3 May 1429: People of Orléans hold processions throughout the city in honour of Jeanne d'Arc.

Evening 2 May 1429: Jeanne d'Arc prays in the Cathedral of Sainte-Croix.

Morning (?) 4 May 1429: Dunois returns from Blois with additional troops, along with La Hire and other leaders, and enters Orléans through the Burgundy Gate: Jeanne d'Arc rides out to meet them; the English in the Boulevard Saint-Loup do not try to intercept this column.

ST. LADRE

1 May 1429: Dunois goes to Blois (via the ferry at Checy) to confer with the Comte de Clermont and collect troops assembling there; Jeanne d'Arc and her companions ride around the streets of Orléans, meeting and encouraging the people.

ILE AUX BOEUFS

C

ST. LOUP

9

A

Afternoon 4 May 1429: French attack the English Boulevard de Saint-Loup; Jeanne d'Arc joins the attack after it has started; the French drive off an attempted English counter-attack from the Boulevard de Saint-Pouair in support of the Boulevard de Saint-Loup, and take the Boulevard de Saint-Loup after three hours fighting; the French then demolish the Boulevard de Saint-Loup.

PORT SAINT-LOUP

ILE SAINT-LOUP

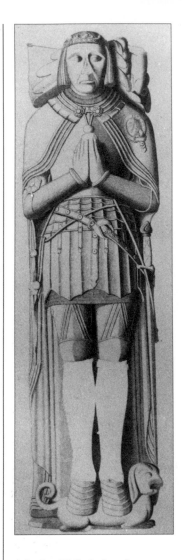

John Lord Talbot played a prominent though not very successful role during the English siege of Orléans. He later became the Earl of Shrewsbury and was one of the leading commanders during the last years of the Hundred Years War. His somewhat battered effigy in Whitchurch church, Shropshire was made around 1455 and has him wearing the most modern armour of the mid-15th century. (ex-C.A. Stothard, *Monumental Effigies of Great Britain*, 1817)

to the city while himself moving to Gien with a large force. Nevertheless, a month elapsed before the French retook Jargeau. This may have been because they had suffered heavy losses during the siege of Orléans or that so many troops had left after the siege. Jeanne d'Arc had also been wounded. Certainly Dunois and other captains went to Charles VII to raise more men and money. English movements in Paris clearly dominated French thinking. There was also a division of opinion about whether the French should attack English-held Normandy or should clear up the Loire. After Charles VII held a council of war early in June, the latter course was adopted.

The French retake the Loire castles

On 8 June a substantial English force commanded by Fastolf finally left Paris, but it advanced slowly and stopped at Janville. It seems unlikely that Jeanne d'Arc's reputation could have yet undermined English morale. Fastolf also enjoyed a reputation for success and is thought to have had around 4,000 men under his command. But these were of

secondary quality drawn from various English garrisons and were accompanied by French troops of doubtful loyalty.

Two days after Fastolf left Paris, Jeanne d'Arc and a French force under the Duc d'Alençon well equipped with cannon left Orléans and headed for Jargeau. They arrived on the 11th. Though Alençon was in command, he now seems to have followed Jeanne's advice in military matters. Jargeau was on the southern side of the Loire and although much smaller than Orléans was strongly fortified with a suburb outside the wall and fortified bridge. The English garrison numbered 300 to 400 men plus a local militia who were expected to help their occupiers. The English also had plenty of guns and were commanded by Suffolk, assisted by two of his brothers. Jeanne inevitably advised a direct assault and so the French attacked the suburbs. The English were unwilling to lose even these and so came out of their fortifications to fight. The French fell back but Jeanne took her banner and led a counter-attack which secured the suburb and bridge. She then warned the English to

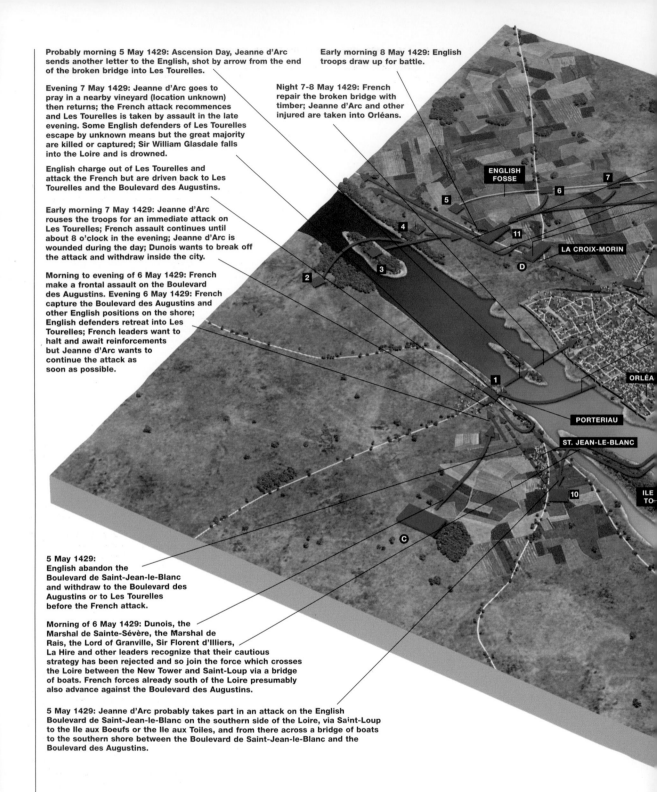

Probably morning 5 May 1429: Ascension Day, Jeanne d'Arc sends another letter to the English, shot by arrow from the end of the broken bridge into Les Tourelles.

Evening 7 May 1429: Jeanne d'Arc goes to pray in a nearby vineyard (location unknown) then returns; the French attack recommences and Les Tourelles is taken by assault in the late evening. Some English defenders of Les Tourelles escape by unknown means but the great majority are killed or captured; Sir William Glasdale falls into the Loire and is drowned.

English charge out of Les Tourelles and attack the French but are driven back to Les Tourelles and the Boulevard des Augustins.

Early morning 7 May 1429: Jeanne d'Arc rouses the troops for an immediate attack on Les Tourelles; French assault continues until about 8 o'clock in the evening; Jeanne d'Arc is wounded during the day; Dunois wants to break off the attack and withdraw inside the city.

Morning to evening of 6 May 1429: French make a frontal assault on the Boulevard des Augustins. Evening 6 May 1429: French capture the Boulevard des Augustins and other English positions on the shore; English defenders retreat into Les Tourelles; French leaders want to halt and await reinforcements but Jeanne d'Arc wants to continue the attack as soon as possible.

Early morning 8 May 1429: English troops draw up for battle.

Night 7-8 May 1429: French repair the broken bridge with timber; Jeanne d'Arc and other injured are taken into Orléans.

ENGLISH FOSSE

LA CROIX-MORIN

ORLÉA

PORTERIAU

ST. JEAN-LE-BLANC

ILE TO-

5 May 1429: English abandon the Boulevard de Saint-Jean-le-Blanc and withdraw to the Boulevard des Augustins or to Les Tourelles before the French attack.

Morning of 6 May 1429: Dunois, the Marshal de Sainte-Sévère, the Marshal de Rais, the Lord of Granville, Sir Florent d'Illiers, La Hire and other leaders recognize that their cautious strategy has been rejected and so join the force which crosses the Loire between the New Tower and Saint-Loup via a bridge of boats. French forces already south of the Loire presumably also advance against the Boulevard des Augustins.

5 May 1429: Jeanne d'Arc probably takes part in an attack on the English Boulevard de Saint-Jean-le-Blanc on the southern side of the Loire, via Saint-Loup to the Ile aux Boeufs or the Ile aux Toiles, and from there across a bridge of boats to the southern shore between the Boulevard de Saint-Jean-le-Blanc and the Boulevard des Augustins.

SIEGE OF ORLÉANS

5–8 May 1429, viewed from the south-west, showing the series of French attacks that capture the English siege positions south of the Loire. When Les Tourelles is also captured the English abandon the siege of Orléans.

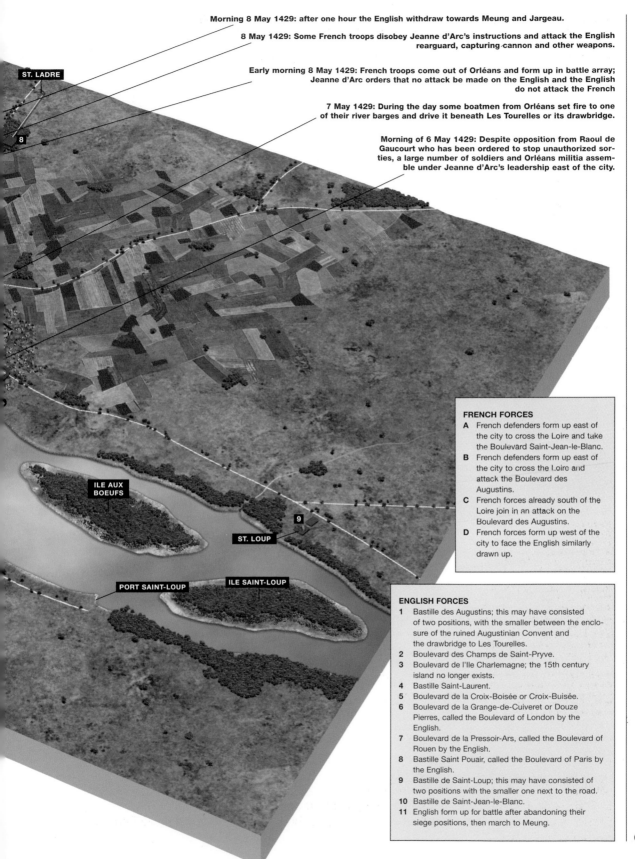

Morning 8 May 1429: after one hour the English withdraw towards Meung and Jargeau.

8 May 1429: Some French troops disobey Jeanne d'Arc's instructions and attack the English rearguard, capturing cannon and other weapons.

Early morning 8 May 1429: French troops come out of Orléans and form up in battle array; Jeanne d'Arc orders that no attack be made on the English and the English do not attack the French

7 May 1429: During the day some boatmen from Orléans set fire to one of their river barges and drive it beneath Les Tourelles or its drawbridge.

Morning of 6 May 1429: Despite opposition from Raoul de Gaucourt who has been ordered to stop unauthorized sorties, a large number of soldiers and Orléans militia assemble under Jeanne d'Arc's leadership east of the city.

ST. LADRE

8

ILE AUX BOEUFS

9

ST. LOUP

PORT SAINT-LOUP

ILE SAINT-LOUP

FRENCH FORCES

A French defenders form up east of the city to cross the Loire and take the Boulevard Saint-Jean-le-Blanc.

B French defenders form up east of the city to cross the Loire and attack the Boulevard des Augustins.

C French forces already south of the Loire join in an attack on the Boulevard des Augustins.

D French forces form up west of the city to face the English similarly drawn up.

ENGLISH FORCES

1 Bastille des Augustins; this may have consisted of two positions, with the smaller between the enclosure of the ruined Augustinian Convent and the drawbridge to Les Tourelles.

2 Boulevard des Champs de Saint-Pryve.

3 Boulevard de l'Ile Charlemagne; the 15th century island no longer exists.

4 Bastille Saint-Laurent.

5 Boulevard de la Croix-Boisée or Croix-Buisée.

6 Boulevard de la Grange-de-Cuiveret or Douze Pierres, called the Boulevard of London by the English.

7 Boulevard de la Pressoir-Ars, called the Boulevard of Rouen by the English.

8 Bastille Saint Pouair, called the Boulevard of Paris by the English.

9 Bastille de Saint-Loup; this may have consisted of two positions with the smaller one next to the road.

10 Bastille de Saint-Jean-le-Blanc.

11 English form up for battle after abandoning their siege positions, then march to Meung.

surrender or be massacred. Again the English refused, though without insults or mockery this time.

French guns now bombarded the fortifications from both sides of the river while the English replied. In addition to some guns which had been inside Orléans, the French were using cannon which the English had abandoned. Meanwhile the English guns were clearly effective and nearly killed the Duc d'Alençon, as he himself recalled during Jeanne's rehabilitation trial: *During the attack on the town of Jargeau, Jeanne told me at one moment to retire from the place where I was at, for if I did not retire from that place that machine – and she pointed to a piece of artillery in the town – will kill you. I fell back and a little later on that very spot where I had been standing someone by the name of my lord Du Lude was killed … That made me very much afraid, and I wondered greatly at Jeanne's saying after all these events.*

Soon, however, a large French bombard named the Bergérie brought down a large tower, whereupon Suffolk started to negotiate with La Hire – much to the annoyance of Alençon, who ordered La Hire to break off contact. The following morning, 12 June, the French launched a direct assault during which the *culverin* of Jean le Cannonier was again highly effective, picking off the best of the defenders. During the attack Jeanne d'Arc was struck on her helmet by a large stone and knocked to the ground, but she picked herself up and urged the men forward. The place was stormed and around 300 English troops were killed, a large number being executed after the town fell. Their leaders were, as usual, taken prisoner. These included Suffolk and one of his brothers, the

Part of the battlefield of Patay seen from the road between Coinces and Lignarolles looking north-east towards the possible location of the English camp. The picture is taken from the site of the medieval road junction which is believed to have been the focal point of the battle. (author's photograph)

other being killed. In fact the Earl of Suffolk was so appalled at being captured by a mere squire that he knighted the man before permitting himself to be taken.

Jeanne d'Arc now returned to Orléans, where she must have learned that Fastolf had established his camp on Les Plaines de la Beauce, near fortified Janville. So the French decision to next attack Beaugency and Meung was a daring one. But perhaps they were aware of low morale and uncertainty within Fastolf's camp. In fact it took the French three days to reorganise and bring their artillery back from Jargeau before setting out against Meung. Some of their heavier guns seem to have been shipped down the Loire by boat. The castle of Meung, where Talbot and Scales had installed their troops, was a little way from the town while the town was separated by a broad meadow from the bridge where some weak fortifications had been added by the English. Presumably this was why the French only attacked and took the bridge on 15 June. Ignoring both the town and the castle, they crossed to the north bank, left a strong force to hold the bridge and marched south towards Beaugency. Here the English garrison abandoned the town and concentrated their forces in a strong castle that dominated another bridge over the Loire. Talbot and perhaps Scales now hurried north to join Fastolf, if they had not already done so a few days earlier, and Talbot demanded revenge for the English failure at Orléans. He insisted that all available troops march to the immediate relief of Meung and Beaugency. Fastolf still advised caution but when Talbot started off on his own, Fastolf felt obliged to follow on 16 June.

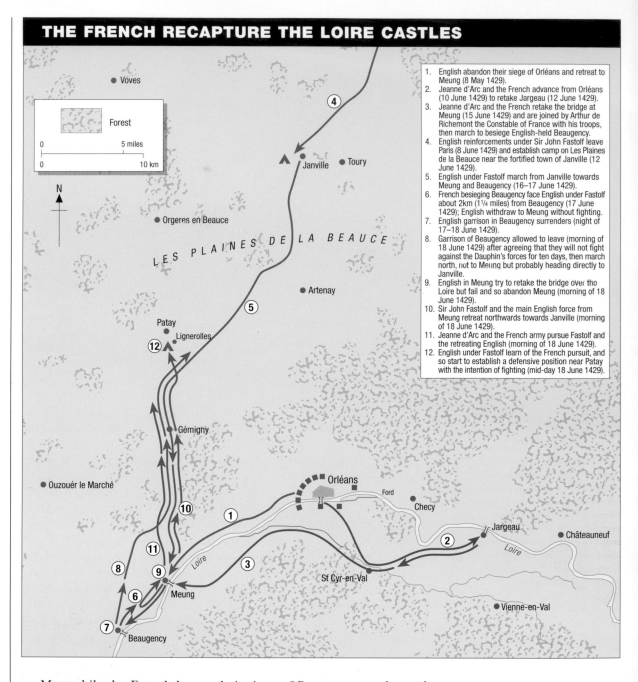

1. English abandon their siege of Orléans and retreat to Meung (8 May 1429).
2. Jeanne d'Arc and the French advance from Orléans (10 June 1429) to retake Jargeau (12 June 1429).
3. Jeanne d'Arc and the French retake the bridge at Meung (15 June 1429) and are joined by Arthur de Richemont the Constable of France with his troops, then march to besiege English-held Beaugency.
4. English reinforcements under Sir John Fastolf leave Paris (8 June 1429) and establish camp on Les Plaines de la Beauce near the fortified town of Janville (12 June 1429).
5. English under Fastolf march from Janville towards Meung and Beaugency (16–17 June 1429).
6. French besieging Beaugency face English under Fastolf about 2km (1¼ miles) from Beaugency (17 June 1429); English withdraw to Meung without fighting.
7. English garrison in Beaugency surrenders (night of 17–18 June 1429).
8. Garrison of Beaugency allowed to leave (morning of 18 June 1429) after agreeing that they will not fight against the Dauphin's forces for ten days, then march north, not to Meung but probably heading directly to Janville.
9. English in Meung try to retake the bridge over the Loire but fail and so abandon Meung (morning of 18 June 1429).
10. Sir John Fastolf and the main English force from Meung retreat northwards towards Janville (morning of 18 June 1429).
11. Jeanne d'Arc and the French army pursue Fastolf and the retreating English (morning of 18 June 1429).
12. English under Fastolf learn of the French pursuit, and so start to establish a defensive position near Patay with the intention of fighting (mid-day 18 June 1429).

Meanwhile the French began their siege of Beaugency castle on the 17th. At this point Arthur de Richemont, the disgraced former Constable of France, arrived from Brittany with around 1,000 men-at-arms and archers. This caused a problem. Should his offer of help be accepted or should he be spurned with the risk that he might join the English? Richemont was still in disgrace but he was a highly esteemed commander. Jeanne d'Arc and Alençon were initially unwilling to accept him, but La Hire and other captains argued in his favour. According to Guillaume Gruel, writing from the Breton point of view, Richemont said to Jeanne: *It has been said that you wish to fight with me. I do not know if you are from God or not. If you are from God, I do not fear you because God knows my good will. If*

ABOVE **The siege and relief of Orléans were naturally popular subjects in late 15th-century French art. Here the English are shown attacking the city in 1429, using cannon, longbows and a crossbow. Their siege-works are shown as substantial timber towers. (*Les Vigiles de Roi Charles VII* by Martial d'Auvergne, Bib. Nationale, Ms. Fr. 5054, Paris).**

RIGHT **Jeanne d'Arc (right) and Judith holding the head of Holofernes in the oldest surviving manuscript illustration of Jeanne, made by Martin le Franc in Arras in 1451. (*Champion des Dames* , Bib. Royale, Ms. 9466, Brussels)**

TOP **Part of the battlefield of Patay from the road between Coinces and Lignarolles looking north-west towards the village of Lignarolles. The English attempted to establish their main position on this slope. (author's photograph)**

ABOVE **'The Virgin Mary and the Powers' on a panel painting from the alterpiece of Albrecht II, south German, 1438. Apart from the varied arms and armour of the figures accompanying the Virgin, armour and weapons are hung on the wall between them. (*in situ* Klosterneuburg)**

ABOVE **The shallow valley of the Retrêve was partially obstructed with thickets and tangled shrubs at the time of the battle of Patay. Here the English attempted to establish their forward position. (author's photograph)**

LEFT **The valley of the Retrêve, seen here on the right looking south-east from the site of the medieval crossroads, is so shallow that it presented no real obstacle to the French cavalry under La Hire. It was approximately in this location that Talbot established the English first line (Author's photograph)**

you are from the devil I fear you even less. Nevertheless the resulting reconciliation may have alienated some leaders. Arthur de Richemont's contingent, as the last to arrive at the siege, was charged with keeping watch on the enemy the following night.

Fastolf and Talbot also reached the Loire on 17 June. He now had between 4,000 and 5,000 men which was probably a few more than the French. After arriving at Meung the English did not immediately attack the French-held bridge but pressed on towards Beaugency. Their vanguard was, in fact, commanded by Charles de la Ramée and Pierre Baugé who were Frenchmen of the pro-English or Lancastrian faction. They marched along a small river called the Mauve, which ran alongside the Loire. About four kilometres (2¹/₂miles) from Beaugency the road crossed a small dip called 'Les Vallées' then rose steeply towards the plateau. Here the French army had assembled when they heard of the English approach. Positioned on top of the slope they blocked the road

The defenders of Orléans attack one of the surrounding English siege-works in a late 15th-century French manuscript. (*Les Vigiles de Roi Charles VII* by Martial d'Auvergne, Bib. Nationale, Ms. Fr. 5054, Paris)

RIGHT **Jeanne d'Arc in full armour with her banner showing various saints, in a mid- to late-15th century Franco-Flemish manuscript. (Archives Nationales, Paris)**

Et d'autres anglois belle bille.
En gaignant la .pour leur estrame.
De beauly efais cinquante mille.

LA HIRE
ET POTON

Coment la hire et poton pour leur
vaillance faient fais cappitaines.

while Richemont and his Bretons continued the bombardment of Beaugency. As night approached, English heralds challenged the French to come down and fight but the latter declined and the two sides drew back to Meung and Beaugency respectively.

According to the Chronicles of Enguerrand de Montstrelet: *The chief English captains in Beaugency saw that this Maiden's fame had completely turned their own fortune, causing them to lose several towns and fortresses which had gone over to the enemy, some by attack and conquest, others by private agreement. Moreover, their men were mostly in a sorry state of fear and seemed to have lost their usual prudence in action. They wanted to withdraw into Normandy and their leaders did not know what to advise or to do, since they did not even know when or whether their reinforcements were likely to arrive.* In fact the withdrawal of Fastolf and Talbot led the garrison in Beaugency to conclude that they had been abandoned. So their commanders Richard Guestin and Matthew Gough negotiated a surrender in return for being allowed to march with their arms and baggage to Normandy. They also promised not to fight against Charles VII's forces for ten days.

At around 7.00am on 18 June the English left Beaugency and headed north towards Janville. An hour later the French took over. Alençon had also sent men to support the troops holding the bridge at Meung who had been under cannon-fire all night in what may have been one of the first night bombardments in the history of firearms. Apparently the English in Meung hoped to retake the bridge and send troops to support Beaugency from the south bank. After hearing mass, Fastolf and Talbot gathered their men to attack the bridge but when they heard that Beaugency had surrendered, and that the French were preparing to move against Meung, the English commanders decided to abandoned this last position on the Loire and reassemble their forces at Janville. They did not, however, apparently expect to be pursued.

THE BATTLE OF PATAY

Even so the 5,000 or so English troops plus non-combatants took the usual precautions. Their vanguard was commanded by an unnamed English knight with a white banner. Then came the baggage train followed by the main body under Fastolf, Talbot and others including the leaders of pro-Lancastrian French troops. The commander of the English rearguard is unknown. The French did, however, pursue with every intention of forcing a battle. Speed was essential and the French seem to have been strengthened by a stream of new volunteers as a result of their recent successes, eventually numbering almost 6,000 men.

Nevertheless many experienced French captains maintained that the English were invincible if allowed to establish a proper defensive position and this concern dominated their tactics during the pursuit. The French advanced quickly but with extreme care so that they did not bump into the English in a disorderly manner. They also hoped to catch the English before they had a chance to adopt a proper defensive posture. So a large all-cavalry vanguard of around 1,500 elite men-at-arms were assembled under the command of Marshal de Boussac, La Hire and Poton de Xaintrailles, with a few dozen scouts riding ahead. This cavalry force also included Beaumanoir, Ambroise de Loré,

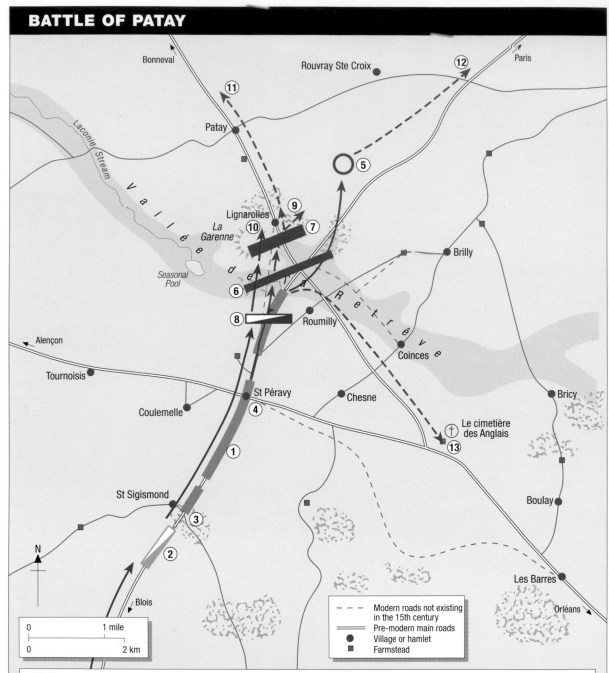

BATTLE OF PATAY

Bonneval

Rouvray Ste Croix

Paris

⑪

⑫

Patay

⑤

Laconie Stream

V a l l é e

⑨

Lignarolles

⑩   ⑦

La Garenne

Brilly

Seasonal Pool

d e

l a   R e t r i e v e

⑥

⑧   Roumilly

Coinces

Alençon

Bricy

Tournoisis

St Péravy

Chesne

④

Coulemelle

Le cimetière des Anglais

Boulay

⑬

①

N

③

St Sigismond

②

Les Barres

Blois

Orléans

	Modern roads not existing in the 15th century
	Pre-modern main roads
●	Village or hamlet
■	Farmstead

0 ——— 1 mile
0 ——— 2 km

---

1. The English army retreating from Meung towards Janville is strung out along the main Blois to Paris road; the baggage train with a small vanguard, then the main force and finally a strong rearguard.
2. The strong French vanguard of cavalry under La Hire pursuing the English are several kilometres ahead of the main French force under Alençon with Jeanne d'Arc.
3. The French vanguard startles a stag which runs into the English rearguard who, not realising that the French are so close, start shouting and chasing the stag. This betrays their presence within a wooded area to the French who promptly attack and disperse the disorganised English rearguard.
4. The English commanders, having confirmed the presence of the French, look for a suitable defensive position.

5. The English baggage train seeks refuge in woods or on a hill north-west of Lignerolles.
6. An elite force of English archers and dismounted men-at-arms, probably under the command of Talbot, tries to establish a first defensive line amongst thickets on either side of the main crossroads.
7. The main English force under Fastolf starts to establish a position on the hill of La Garenne south-west of Lignerolles.
8. La Hire and the French cavalry vanguard immediately forms up, attacks and overwhelms the English infantry in the thickets.
9. Fastolf considers advancing to help Talbot at the crossroads but is persuaded that the day is lost. His men begin to panic because they do not have time to establish a proper defensive position. Those still

mounted start to flee, abandoning those already dismounted.
10. La Hire and the French cavalry vanguard press on with their attack and disperse the English main force on La Garenne.
11. Some English fugitives try to escape north-west towards Chartres; Talbot is captured, probably near Patay.
12. The main group of English fugitives flee north-east towards Janville which closes its gates to them. Fastolf and the mounted fugitives reach Etampes at one o'clock in the morning the following day.
13. Some English fugitives try to escape to the south-east, perhaps towards the Forest of Orléans. Many are apparently slaughtered at a place subsequently known as 'Le cimetière des Anglais'.

Panassac, Giraud de la Pallière and other famous soldiers. The main body, including the infantry, followed as closely as possible under the command of Alençon, Richemont, Dunois and Gilles de Rais – later made infamous as the fictional 'Bluebeard'. Jeanne d'Arc remained with them, along with the Sires de Gaucourt, de Laval and de Lohéac. The role of the vanguard was to catch the English and stop them establishing a strong position, while also looking for ambushes. Jeanne d'Arc was unhappy about such tactics, the more so because she was not with the vanguard. The army thus set off from Beaugency up the valley of the Mauve.

The English marched for about four hours. It was a hot day and around midday, some way south of Patay, Fastolf received a report that the French were in close pursuit. The exact position of the resulting battle is not known for certain. Patay was a Benedictine monastery founded in the 10th or 11th century, around which a small village had developed. Its church also seems to have been fortified. This was a poor region of France consisting of woods and sheep pastures lying between the forest of Orléans to the south and the prosperous Beauce area to the north. Woods and undulations probably limited the view while the forest of Orléans may then have reached as far at Gémigny. One local feature which played a significant role was a crossroads about one kilometre ($^1/_2$mile) south-east of the hamlet of Lignerolles. Here the region's two medieval main roads met and there seems little doubt that Fastolf and Talbot were heading for this junction. The old Blois to Paris road now

TOP **Part of the battlefield of Patay from the road between Coinces and Lignarolles looking south towards the hamlet of Roumilly. The French cavalry vanguard would probably have approached from this direction. The picture is taken from the medieval road junction at the centre of the battlefield. (author's photograph)**

ABOVE **A mounted man-at-arms, probably representing the Duke of Burgundy, rides down his infantry foes. This was exactly what happened when the French cavalry vanguard attacked the dismounted English at the battle of Patay. (in situ Hotel de Ville, Leuven; author's photograph)**

only exists as farm tracks while that between Orléans and Chartres is now partly farm tracks, partly modern road. The crossroads itself is still visible and has a stone commemorating the battle of 1429.

The precise sequence of events is again unclear, with different sources providing conflicting evidence. Nevertheless, a logical interpretation is possible, and seems to run as follows. When the French scouts made contact with the rear of the long English column, the head of this column may have been four to five kilometres ($2^1/2$–3 miles) south-east of Patay, entering the broad but shallow valley of the Retrève. According to Montstrelet: *Prior to the battle of Patay, Jacques de Milly, Gilles de St. Simon, Louis de Marconnay, Jean de la Haye and other valiant men were made knights by the French.* This suggests some pause, but it is not clear whether it applied to the cavalry vanguard or the main French force. Then there is the extraordinary story of the stag.

French scouts came upon the English rearguard while it was on the plateau in a wood and did not see the French. This appears to have happened near the village or castle of Saint-Sigismond which had a pro-English garrison. Apparently the French horsemen startled a stag which was in a copse. This ran into the English rearguard and, because a stag was such a great prize, the English shouted and pursued the animal, not knowing the French were so close. As a result the English rearguard fell into disorder while their shouting warned the French of their presence. La Hire sent a messenger to inform the French main force and then, in accordance with his instructions, pressed rapidly ahead. De Montstrelet described what happened next: *The vanguard of the French were impatient for the attack, having lately found the English very slack in their defence, and made so sudden and violent a charge that they [the English] were unable to form themselves in proper order.*

The English rearguard was certainly taken by surprise. Meanwhile the leading English troops stopped and sent messengers back to find out what was going on. These confirmed that the French were very close. So the English commanders hurriedly looked for a suitable defensive

position. Thomas Basin, author of contemporary *Histoire de Charles VII*, described the area around Patay as a 'vaste and spacious plain'. There was no high ground, but in the direction of Patay the English could see thickets and rising ground. So they decided to establish their defences within these feeble obstacles. The English cavalry vanguard formed a sort of line and, according to Monstrelet, some dismounted while other captains regarded this position as inadequate and so galloped on to what they thought was a stronger position half a kilometre ($^1/_3$ mile) further. Other sources seem to indicate that they headed towards a wood that no longer exists, perhaps on or near a low hill called La Garenne just west of Lignarolles. A local tradition gives the name of 'Le Camp' to a spot two kilometres (1$^1/_4$ miles) east of Patay and many historians believe this was where the English established their position. Yet it seems more likely that 'Le Camp' was where the English baggage train was pillaged after the battle.

Enguerrand de Montstrelet's *Chronicles* described the confusion: *The English now knew that the French were at hand, and made their own preparations for battle. Some wanted to take up their positions on foot near a hedge in order to prevent a surprise attack from the rear. Others, however, were not satisfied with this kind of strategy, and said they would find more advantageous ground. They turned around and retreated six or seven hundred yards [548–640m] from their former position which was full of hedges and undergrowth.*

Apparently the English attempted to establish a defensive position near a hamlet, and Lignerolles is the only candidate. The best we can assume is that the bulk of the English troops under Fastolf began to form up on La Garenne while Talbot, with other men-at-arms and 500 'elite archers', formed up amidst the thickets on either side of major crossroads to the south and south-east. The latter now faced the rapidly advancing French vanguard under La Hire. On this occasion the complexity of the traditional English defensive array, including the famous *herce* or harrow formation with sharpened stakes and ditches or potholes, may have betrayed the dismounted English. It took time to

THE BATTLE OF PATAY, 18 JUNE 1429
Patay was not the first time that French forces had defeated the English in open battle during the Hundred Years War. On the other hand the invaders were so totally routed that English morale suffered a serious setback while Jeanne d'Arc's reputation, already high after breaking the siege of Orléans, increased still further. The battle is also interesting because on this oocasion French mounted men-at-arms bowled over the English, who were, as usual, on foot. (Graham Turner)

establish, and time was what the English did not have. Similarly the oft-criticised 'impatience' of French armoured cavalry may have been intended to strike their dismounted foes before the latter were ready.

The main fighting began around 2.00pm and was soon over. La Hire saw his enemy in disorder and, with an audacity which went beyond his orders, attacked at once, dispersing the English 'rear guard' or what should perhaps now be termed their front line. De Montstrelet indicates that many of the French attacked on foot, but elsewhere it seems that the majority of La Hire's vanguard were still mounted. When the first English line collapsed, the larger force under Fastolf's command, probably on the low hill of La Garenne, fell into disorder. They had not yet formed up for battle, although many of the men-at-arms had dismounted. Those still on their horses began to leave the field. Meanwhile the French vanguard came on as fast as it could. Fastolf saw what had happened to Talbot's men and tried to rally his own troops to rescue them, but disorder now turned into panic. Those captains still in their saddles advised Fastolf that the day was lost and that he should not risk further fighting until he got reinforcements from Paris. Whether it was retreat or rout, those English who could do so now fled towards Paris, abandoning those who had dismounted. Those on foot also tried to flee, some seeking refuge in the woods of La Garenne, others in Lignarolles. It was every man for himself and the result was a massacre.

Following Charles VII's coronation in the sacred city of Reims, the Anglo-Burgundian regime attempted to strengthen its position by having the child Henry VI crowned in Paris. Here the infant monarch greets dignitaries outside the walls of Paris, as illustrated in a mid-15th-century French manuscript. (*Chronique de Froissart*, Bib. Nationale, Ms. Fr. 2645, f.321v, Paris)

ABOVE **The hill of La Garenne, topped by trees on the right, seen from a derelict windmill just to the west of Lignarolles. It was here that the English position collapsed and the massacre began. (author's photograph)**

RIGHT **The old mill outside Lignerolles with the village in the background. This is where the fiercest fighting in the battle of Patay took place. (author's photograph)**

Quite when the main French force arrived is again unknown. They were probably quite a long way behind La Hire's vanguard but would have pressed ahead when they heard what was happening. Nevertheless, the real battle was already over and, according to the *Journal du Siège d'Orléans*, the main French army only pursued the fleeing English. Only those worth holding for ransom were made prisoner. The slaughter began around the crossroads, on La Garenne and in Lignerolles. It then continued along the main roads towards Paris, Chartres and back towards Orléans. Here, between six and seven kilometres ($3\frac{3}{4}$–$4\frac{1}{3}$ miles) from the crossroads, was a spot that became known locally as the *cimetière des Anglais*. Perhaps these unfortunates were fleeing south-east towards the shelter of the Forest of Orléans. At Janville, on the road to

Paris, the citizens heard of the English defeat, closed their gates to the fugitives and declared for Charles VII. The same happened along the road towards Chartres and it was in this direction that Talbot was taken prisoner.

After the battle Alençon and most of the leaders including Jeanne d'Arc spent the night in Patay. French casualties had been very light but it was said that around 2,000 English and 'false French' were killed with a further 200 being taken prisoner. According to Montstrelet: *Some eighteen hundred English were left dead on the field, and a hundred or more taken prisoner, among them the Lords Scales, Talbot and Hungerford, Sir Thomas Rempstone and several more. Among the dead were a certain number of the leaders; the rest of the men being of middling or low degree – the sort who are always brought from their own country to die in France.* Fastolf reached Etampes about 1.00am the following morning. Next day he joined the Duke of Bedford in Corbeil. There the Regent took away Fastolf's Order of the Garter, though this was later returned by a tribunal of inquiry. But Talbot, who had been abandoned during Fastolf's attempt to save the English army, never forgave Fastolf.

Near the southern end of the village of Lignerolles there is a typical old French enclosed farmyard. Though the walls and gate are almost certainly later than the 15th century, a farm probably existed here at the time of the battle and English fugitives might well have tried to defend themselves in such a place. (author's photograph)

AFTERMATH AND RECKONING

The battle of Patay was more decisive than the relief of the siege of Orléans. Not only was the only available English field army destroyed but Patay proved that English troops were not invincible in ranged battle. As a result the morale of Charles VII and his supporters rose accordingly. The loss of so many soldiers weakened existing English garrisons while Charles's control over the Loire valley was confirmed. The dream of a combined English and French realm had effectively been destroyed and Jeanne d'Arc now encouraged Charles to lead his army through weakened enemy territory to the sacred city of Reims. Here alone a proper coronation could be conducted and once this was done, Charles VII's legitimacy and prestige rose.

Yet the war was far from over. The Duke of Bedford tried to force Charles VII's army into battle but the French, still somewhat in awe of their famous opponents, avoided a direct confrontation. Charles did, however, permit Jeanne d'Arc to attempt to capture Paris on 8 September 1429. This was a dismal failure, undermining Jeanne's already shaky position at court. Charles and his more cautious, or perhaps more realistic, advisers negotiated a truce with the English. In 1431 the English child-king Henry VI was crowned 'King of France' in Paris, but the ceremony was a pale imitation of Charles's coronation in Reims. By then Jeanne d'Arc had already been captured by the Burgundians and sold to the English. Tried for heresy, she was executed at Rouen in 1431. Meanwhile the English recovered most of their losses in the Seine valley and the French concentrated on attacking Burgundy to undermine the Anglo-Burgundian alliance. In 1435 this alliance collapsed – an event as important as the relief of Orléans, the battle of Patay and the coronation at Reims. Even so French progress remained slow and only in 1449, after a series of major military reforms, could Charles VII launch successful attacks on the English-held regions of France.

The reasons for English failure outside Orléans are not immediately apparent. It was a trial of strength in which, given the nature, size and experience of the two armies, victory could have gone either way. One French captain, Jean de Bueil, who was present at the siege, later wrote a severe critique of English operations in his military handbook *Le Jouvencel*. Above all he criticised the English reliance on fortified siege positions, *boulevards* and *bastilles* where they could not make proper use of cavalry. Furthermore these positions were so separated from each other that they were unable to provide mutual support. The significant role played by cannon encouraged Charles VII to establish a permanent artillery park as soon as he was in a position to do so, and this would play an even more important role in driving the English from France. The Orléans campaign also convinced French commanders finally to abandon the old tactics of frontal assault, at least when an enemy had time to establish a proper defensive position. Instead the French increasingly relied on surprise attacks, ruses and minor operations to wear down their enemy physically and morally.

The English were fully aware that things were not going their way, but Jeanne d'Arc was not necessarily blamed for this sudden change in English fortunes. The 15th-century poet John Lydgate, for example, wrote his *Libelle of Englyshe Polycyr* around this time.

> Now then, for love of Christ and his joy,
>> Bring yet England out of trouble and noye [tribulation].
> Take heart and wit and set at goverance,
>> Set many wittes [minds] withouten variance,
> At one accord and unanimity,
>> Put to good will to keep the sea [maintain control over the sea],
> First for worship and for profit also,
>> And to rebuke of each evil-willed foe.

It is difficult to assess how Jeanne d'Arc was really viewed at the time because her actions were so sanctified by patriotic legend and religious fervour in later centuries. Certainly she was the inspiration of the last known work by that remarkable medieval 'proto-feminist' Christine de Pizan, who wrote her *Ditié de Jeanne d'Arc* shortly after Charles VII was crowned at Reims. This was the first work to celebrate Jeanne and was the only one written during her lifetime. It is also optimistic and passionate; a view repeated by Matthieu Thomassin, who compiled the collection of poems in which Christine's verse is found: *Of all the signs of love sent by God to this realm, there has been none so great nor so marvelous as that Maid.* Though not one of Christine de Pizan's best poems, she wrote:

> What honour this for womankind,
>> Well-loved of God, it would appear,
> When that sad crowd to loss resigned,
>> Fled from the kingdom in great fear
> Now by a woman rescued here
>> Which 5,000 men could not do
> Who made the traitors disappear.
>> One could scarcely believe it true.

Jeanne d'Arc came to be regarded as the most heroic of French saints. More immediately she became a political force after Charles's coronation, leading a faction that favoured continued war against England rather than seeking political negotiations. Military setbacks then destroyed her influence and although Jeanne's family had now been ennobled, she herself was politically isolated.

Her claims to divine guidance and her remarkable battlefield success had already aroused suspicions of sorcery. Following her capture, her trial was used as a means of discrediting the Valois cause. Sentenced to life imprisonment and penance, Jeanne d'Arc relapsed almost as soon as she had regained her strength and was consequently burned at the stake. She remained a controversial figure and so in 1456 Charles VII

Some years after the siege of Orléans, the Duc d'Alençon was accused of treacherous dealings with the English as well as dabbling in black magic. His trial at Vendôme in October 1458, shown here in a contemporary manuscript attributed to the artist Jean Fouquet, marked a significant point in the French king's effort to impose a centralised monarchy on France. (Boccaccio's *De Casibus Virorum Illustrium*, Bayerische Staatsbibliothek, Cod. Gall. g, f.2v, Munich)

arranged the annulment of her conviction, mainly to remove the stigma of his own association with a convicted 'witch'.

Jeanne's influence may also have been exaggerated, though for French historians this view is almost sacrilegious. What Jeanne d'Arc certainly left behind was a story of remarkable success, courage and dedication which became an example for other French soldiers to follow. But if Jeanne really created such dismay amongst France's enemies, surely it would be found in the records. In fact there was little interest in her in England until many years later. By the 16th century her legend had grown and Jeanne d'Arc features prominently in Shakespeare's play *King Henry VI, Part One*. In Scene V, set before one of the gates of Orléans, *La Pucelle* or Jeanne enters driving Englishmen before her. Then Talbot enters and says: *Where is my strength, my valour and my force? Our English troops retire, I cannot stay them; A woman clad in armour chaseth them; Here, here she comes. (Enter La Pucelle) I'll have a bout with thee; Devil or devil's dam, I'll conjour thee: Blood will I draw on thee, – thou art a witch, – And straightway give thy soul to him thou serv'st.* They fight but neither wins. The differing English and French myths of Jeanne d'Arc were established. Even as late as 1817 she was seen in England as a fanatic if not a fraud and Stothard, in his *Monumental Effigies of Great Britain*, summed up English prejudice during the immediate post-Napoleonic period: ... *the siege of Orléans was raised by the celebrated Joan of Arc, styled for her fanatical pretension La Pucelle de Dieu. This gave a temporary turn of success for the French cause* ... What Stothard conveniently forgot, as do many English people to this day, was that France eventually won the Hundred Years War, with the career of Jeanne d'Arc marking the turning point.

THE BATTLEFIELDS TODAY

France is one of the easiest and most pleasant countries to tour, whatever means of transport is used. The Loire Valley with its stunning views and superb castles is also a favourite tourist destination. Hotels of all categories are available and there are plenty of clean, cheap and well-organised camp-sites. Unfortunately Orléans has lost most of its medieval buildings as a result of the Hundred Years War, the French Wars of Religion and German bombing during the Second World War. The existing Cathedral of Sainte-Croix is largely a 17th–18th-century building and the only remaining medieval churches are those of Saint-Pierre (12th–13th century) and Saint-Aignan (15th century), which was rebuilt after the English siege. One tower from the medieval fortifications also survives. The medieval bridge is long gone, though some of its foundations can been seen when the river level is low. The house in which Jeanne d'Arc lived during the siege is also a modern replacement for the original, which was bombed in 1940. Orléans has, of course, grown far beyond its 15th-century limits and although the locations of the surrounding English siege-positions are known, nothing whatever remains of them. A charming square and a discreet monumental cross do, however, mark the site of the fortification of Les Tourelles and the *boulevard* of Les Augustins.

Some of the other Loire towns and castles involved in this campaign have fared better. The castle at Châteauneuf-sur-Loire was rebuilt in the 17th century but even so only a small part remains. Even less remains at Jargeau, but at Meung the much modified 13th-century castle is sometimes open to visitors. In fact the little town or large village with its castle, medieval church and other relics of fortification is very picturesque. The best preserved of all the sites involved in the fighting of 1428–29 is, however, Beaugency. It has been described as 'a picture of the Middle Ages' and has the added advantage of setting its ruined castle-keep, 15th-century château, churches and other historic buildings alongside the Loire with deeply wooded hills rising behind. Chinon, where Jeanne d'Arc was introduced to Charles VII's court, is, of course, one of the most famous locations in the entire historic and beautiful Loire region, while Blois runs a close second.

Fewer visitors travel further north to Châteaudun, where Dunois's garrison held an almost isolated outpost of Valois territory throughout the English invasion of 1428–29, but its castle and old town centre are well worth a visit. Only the dedicated specialist goes further off the beaten track to find the site of the battle of Patay. The surrounding countryside is rather flat and less than scenic but the villages of Lignarolles, Patay and others have the quiet charm so typical of the best French countryside, as do the older walled farms. The wooden windmill that might mark the site of the last English stand has, however, been closed as dangerous and may be due for demolition.

BIBLIOGRAPHY

The castle at Caister in Norfolk was built for Sir John Fastolf who commanded the English at the disastrous battle of Patay. It was also one of the first brick-built castles in England. (photograph Caister Castle Car Collection)

Allmand, C.T., *Society at War, the Experience of England and France during the Hundred Years War* (Edinburgh 1973).

Allmand, C.T., *The Hundred Years War, England and France at War c.1300–c.1450* (Cambridge 1988).

Anon. (edit. F. Guessard & E. de Certain), *Mystère du siège d'Orléans* (Paris 1862).

Anon. (edit. P. Charpentier & C. Cuissard), *Journal du Siège d'Orléans et du voyage de Reims, 1428–29* (Orleans 1896).

Anon., (trans. & edit. D. Rankin & C. Quintail), *The First Biography of Joan of Arc* (Pittsburgh 1964).

Baraude, H., 'Le siége d'Orléans et Jeanne d'Arc, 1428–1429', *Revue des quéstions historiques* LXXX-LXXXI (1906-7) 31–65, 74–112 & 395–424.

Basin, Thomas (edit. & trans. C. Samaran), *Histoire de Charles VII* (Paris 1933).

Boucher de Molandon, M. & Adalbert de Beaucorps, *L'armée anglaise vaincue par Jeanne d'Arc sous les murs d'Orléans* (Orléans 1892).

Burne, A., *The Agincourt War: A Military History of the Latter Part of the Hundred Years War from 1369–1453* (London 1956).

Canonge, Gen. F., *Jeanne d'Arc guerrière* (Paris 1907).

Champion, P., *Jeanne d'Arc* (Paris 1933).

Charpentier, P., *Histoire du siege d'Orléans, 1428–1429* (Orléans 1894).

Chastellain, Georges (edit. Kervyn de Lettenhove), *Oeuvres*, 3 vols. (Brussels 1863–66).

Christine de Pisan (edit. A.J. Kennedy & K. Varty), *Ditié de Jehanne d'Arc* (Oxford 1977).

Collet, LtCol, *Vie militaire de Jeanne d'Arc* (Nancy 1919).

Collin, M., *La casemate du bout du pont des Tourelles a Orléans du côte de la Sologne* (Paris 1867).

Collin, M., *Les derniers jours du pont des Tourelles à Orléans* (Orléans 1875).

Contamine, P., 'Les armées française et anglais à l'époque de Jeanne d'Arc', *Revue des sociétés savantes de haute-normandie. Lettres et sciences humaines* LVII (1970) 5–33.

Contamine, P., 'Le guerre de siège au temps de Jeanne d'Arc', *Dossiers d'archéologie* XXXIV (May 1979) 11–20.

Contamine, P., *Guerres et sociétés en France, en Angleterre et en Bourgogne, XIV–XVe siècle* (Paris 1991).

Cousinot (edit. A. Vallet de Viriville), *Chronique de la Pucelle ou chronique de Cousinot* (Paris 1859).

Debal, J., 'Les fortifications et le pont d'Orléans au temps de Jeanne d'Arc', *Dossiers d'archéologie* XXXIV (May 1979) 77–92.

DeVries, K., 'The Use of Gunpowder Weaponry By and Against Joan of Arc During the Hundred Years War', *War and Society* XIV (1996) 1–16.

Fabre, L. (trans. G. Hopkins), *Joan of Arc* (London 1954).

Févre, Jean Le (edit. F. Morand), *Chronique* (Paris 1881).

Ffoulkes, C., 'The Armour of Jeanne d'Arc', *The Burlington Magazine* XVI (Dec 1909) 141–146.

Jarry, L., 'Deux chansons normandes sur le siège d'Orléans', *Bulletin de la Société archeologique et historique de l'Orleannais*, X (1893) 359–370.

Jarry, L., *Le compte de l'armée anglaise au siège d'Orléans, 1428–1429* (Orléans 1892).

Jeanne d'Arc, une époque, un rayonnement: Colloque d'histoire mediévale, Orléans – Octobre 1979 (Paris 1982).

Lamond, J., *Joan of Arc and England* (London 1927).

Liocourt, F. de, *La Mission de Jeanne d'Arc*, 2 vols. (Paris 1974–76).

Luce, S. (edit), 'Une Pièce de vers sur le siège d'Orléans', in *La France pendant la guerre de cent ans: Episodes historiques et vie privée aux XIVe et XVe siècles* (Paris 1893) 207–214.

Marin, P., *Jeanne d'Arc tacticien et stratégiste: L'art militaire dans la premiere moitié du XVe siècle*, 4 vols. (Paris 1889–90).

Michel de Lombares, 'Patay, 18 Juin 1429', *Revue historique de l'armée* XXII (1966) 5–16.

Michelet, J., *Joan of Arc* (Ann Arbor 1957).

Monstrelet (trans. T. Johnes), *The Chronicles of Enguerrant de Monstrelet* (London 1845).

Murray, T. (edit.), *Jeanne d'Arc, Maid of Orléans* (London 1907).

Olivier, R., 'La lance, l'épée et la hache (les armes de la Pucelle)', *Les amis de Jeanne d'Arc* XLII/3 (1995) 14–21.

Pernoud, R., *Joan of Arc by Herself and Her Witnesses* (New York 1964).

Pernoud, R., *La libération d'Orléans, 8 mai 1429* (Paris 1969).

Quicherat, J., *Histoire du siège d'Orléans et des honneurs rendus a la Pucelle* (Paris 1854).

Sackville-West, V., *Saint Joan of Arc* (London 1936).

Sermoise, P. De, *Joan of Arc and her Secret Missions* (London 1970).

Stolpe, S. (trans. E. Lewenhaupt), *The Maid of Orleans* (London 1956).

Thibault, J., 'Un prince territorial au XVe siècle: Dunois, Bâtard d'Orléans', *Bulletin de la société archéologiques et historiques de l'Orléanais*, n.s. XIV (1997) 3–46.

Vale, M.G.A., *Charles VII* (London 1974).

Vergnaud-Romangnesi, M., *Notice historique sur le fort des Tourelles de l'ancient pont de la ville d'Orléans, ou Jeanne d'Arc combattit et fut blessé, sur la decouverte de ses restes en juillet 1831* (Paris 1832).

Villaret, A. de, *Campagnes des Anglais dans l'Orléanais, la Beauce Chartrain et le Gatinais (1421–1428): L'armée sous Warwick et Suffolk au siège de Montargis. Campagnes de Jeanne d'Arc sur la Loire posterierures au siège d'Orléans* (Orléans 1893).

Warner, M., *Joan of Arc, The Image of Female Heroism* (London 1981).

INDEX

COMPANION SERIES FROM OSPREY

ESSENTIAL HISTORIES
Concise studies of the motives, methods and repercussions of human conflict, spanning history from ancient times to the present day. Each volume studies one major war or arena of war, providing an indispensable guide to the fighting itself, the people involved, and its lasting impact on the world around it.

MEN-AT-ARMS
The uniforms, equipment, insignia, history and organisation of the world's military forces from earliest times to the present day. Authoritative text and full-colour artwork, photographs and diagrams bring over 5000 years of history vividly to life.

ELITE
This series focuses on uniforms, equipment, insignia and unit histories in the same way as Men-at-Arms but in more extended treatments of larger subjects, also including personalities and techniques of warfare.

NEW VANGUARD
The design, development, operation and history of the machinery of warfare through the ages. Photographs, full-colour artwork and cutaway drawings support detailed examinations of the most significant mechanical innovations in the history of human conflict.

ORDER OF BATTLE
The greatest battles in history, featuring unit-by-unit examinations of the troops and their movements as well as analysis of the commanders' original objectives and actual achievements. Colour maps including a large fold-out base map, organisational diagrams and photographs help the reader to trace the course of the fighting in unprecedented detail.

WARRIOR
Insights into the daily lives of history's fighting men and women, past and present, detailing their motivation, training, tactics, weaponry and experiences. Meticulously researched narrative and full-colour artwork, photographs, and scenes of battle and daily life provide detailed accounts of the experiences of combatants through the ages.

AIRCRAFT OF THE ACES
Portraits of the elite pilots of the 20th century's major air campaigns, including unique interviews with surviving aces. Unit listings, scale plans and full-colour artwork combine with the best archival photography available to provide a detailed insight into the experience of war in the air.

COMBAT AIRCRAFT
The world's greatest military aircraft and combat units and their crews, examined in detail. Each exploration of the leading technology, men and machines of aviation history is supported by unit listings and other data, artwork, scale plans, and archival photography.

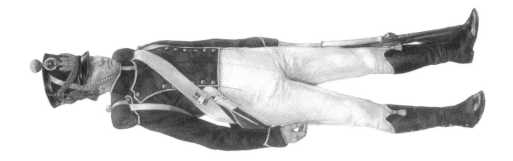

OSPREY
PUBLISHING

FIND OUT MORE ABOUT OSPREY

❑ Please send me a FREE trial issue
   of Osprey Military Journal

❑ Please send me the latest listing of Osprey's publications

❑ I would like to subscribe to Osprey's e-mail newsletter

Title/rank _____

Name _____

Address _____

_____

_____

Postcode/zip _____ state/country _____

e-mail _____

Which book did this card come from?

_____

❑ I am interested in military history

My preferred period of military history is _____

❑ I am interested in military aviation

My preferred period of military aviation is _____

I am interested in *(please tick all that apply)*

❑ general history   ❑ militaria   ❑ model making

❑ wargaming   ❑ re-enactment

Please send to:

USA & Canada: Osprey Direct USA, c/o Motorbooks
International, P.O. Box 1, 729 Prospect Avenue, Osceola,
WI 54020

UK, Europe and rest of world:
Osprey Direct UK, P.O. Box 140, Wellingborough, Northants,
NN8 2FA, United Kingdom

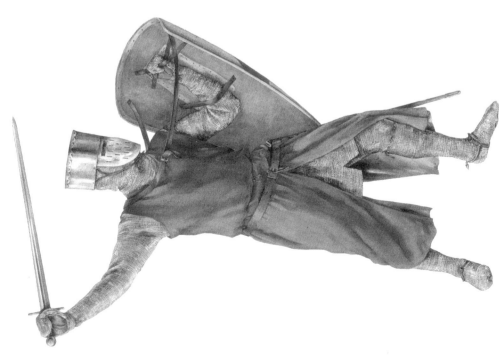

www.ospreypublishing.com

call our telephone hotline
for a free information pack

USA & Canada: 1-800-458-0454
UK, Europe and rest of world call:
+44 (0) 1933 443 863

Young Guardsman
Figure taken from *Warrior 22:
Imperial Guardsman 1799–1815*
Published by Osprey
Illustrated by Christa Hook

Knight, c.1190
Figure taken from *Warrior 1: Norman Knight 950 – 1204AD*
Published by Osprey
Illustrated by Christa Hook

POSTCARD